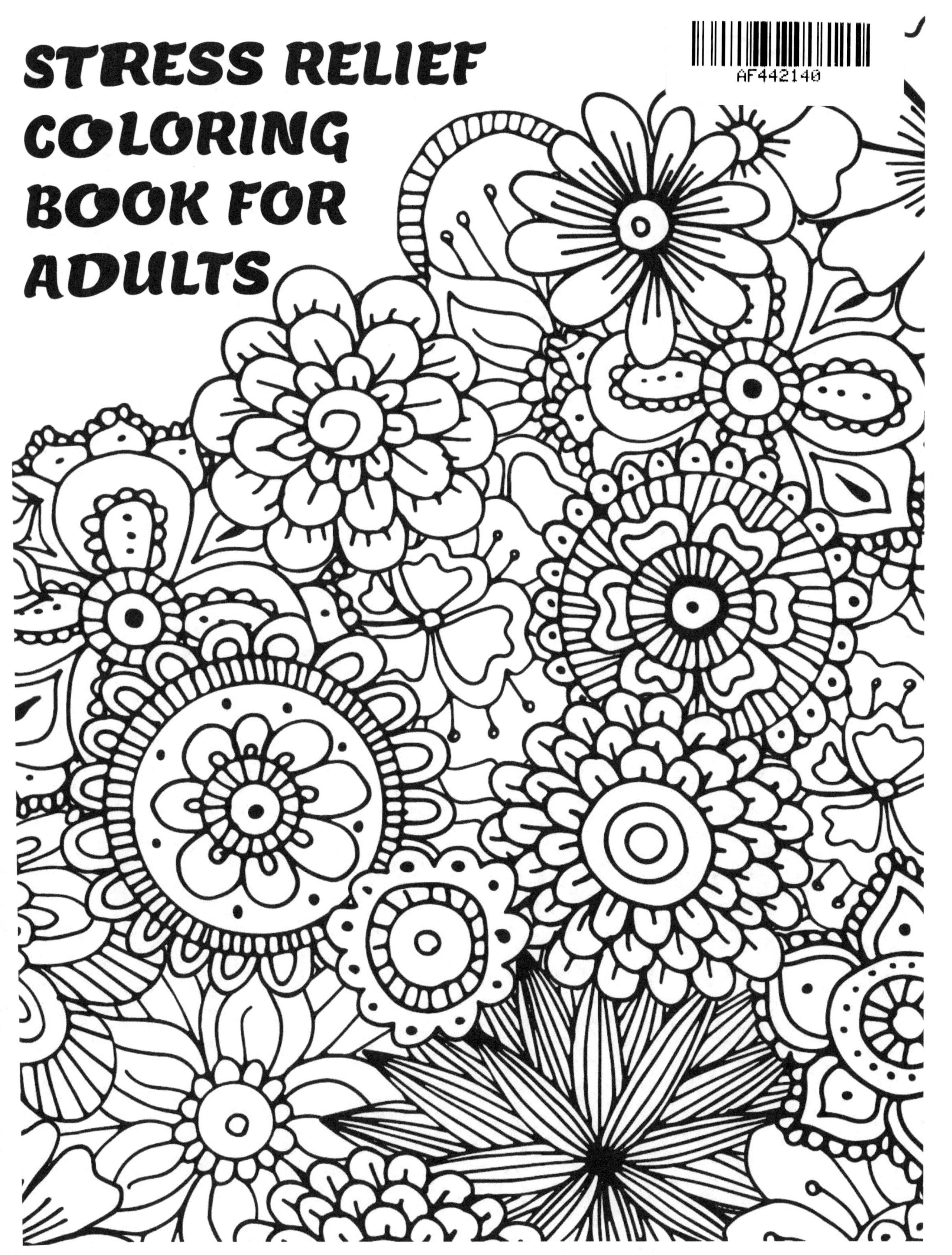
STRESS RELIEF COLORING BOOK FOR ADULTS
AF442140

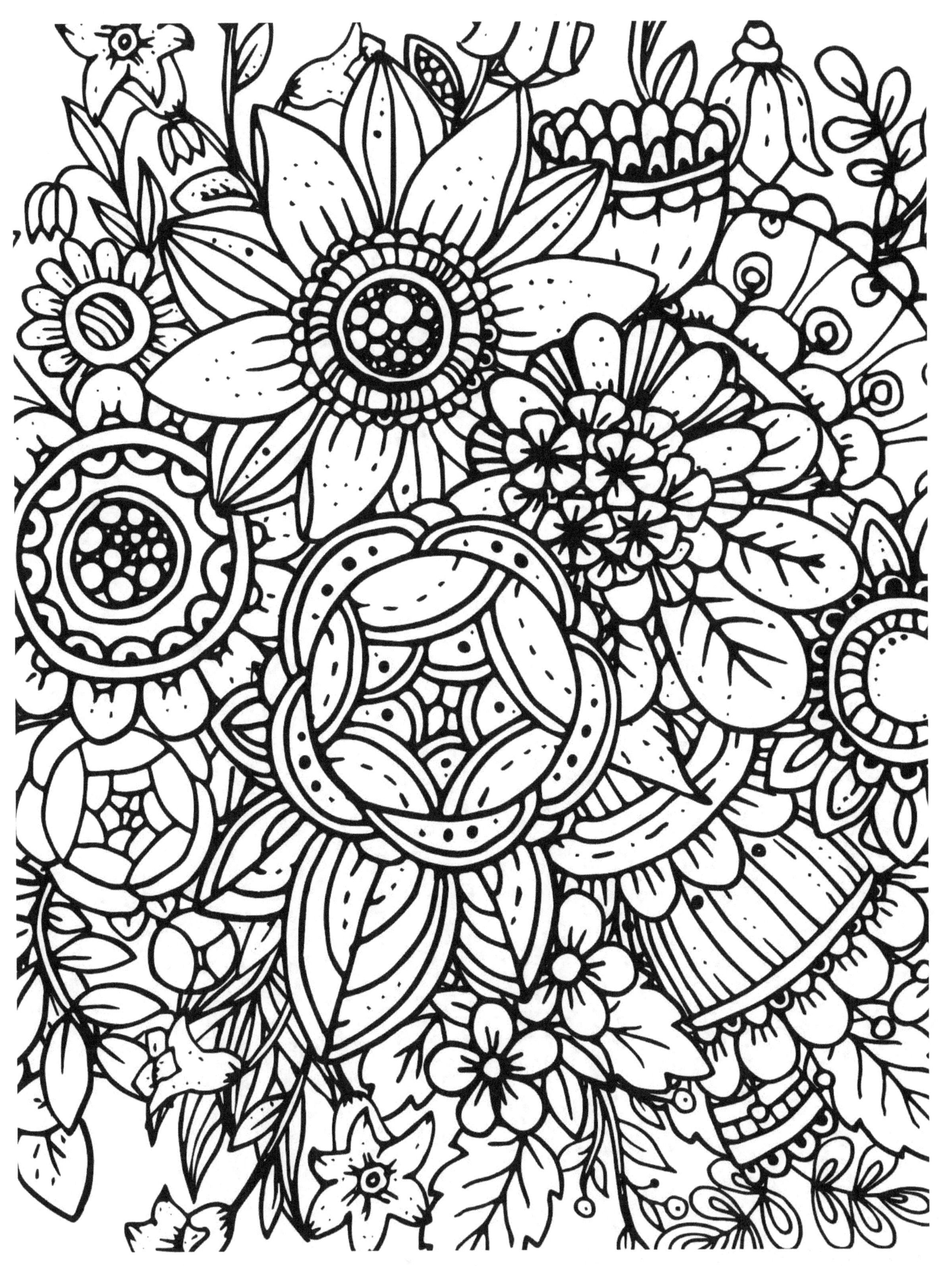

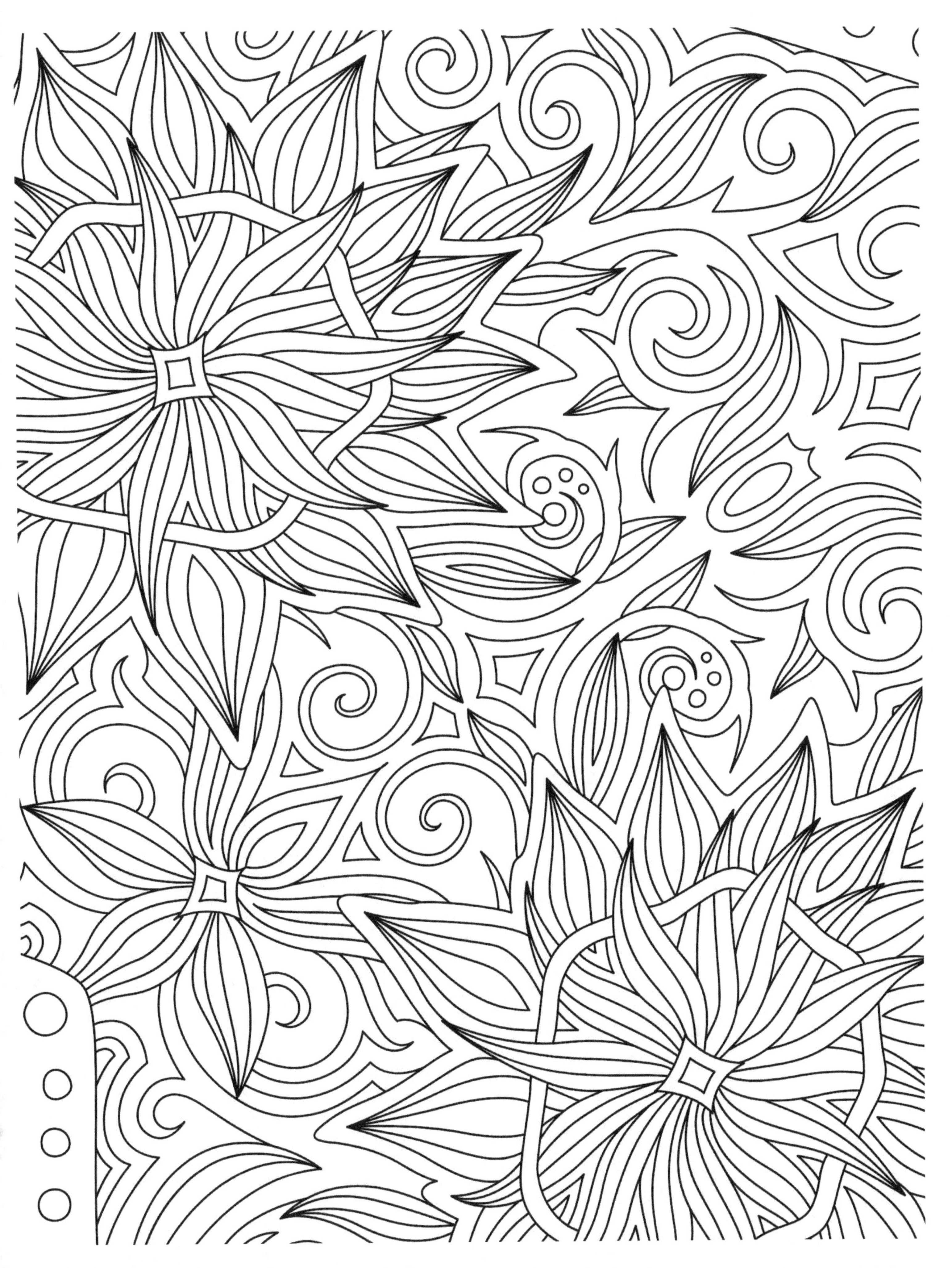

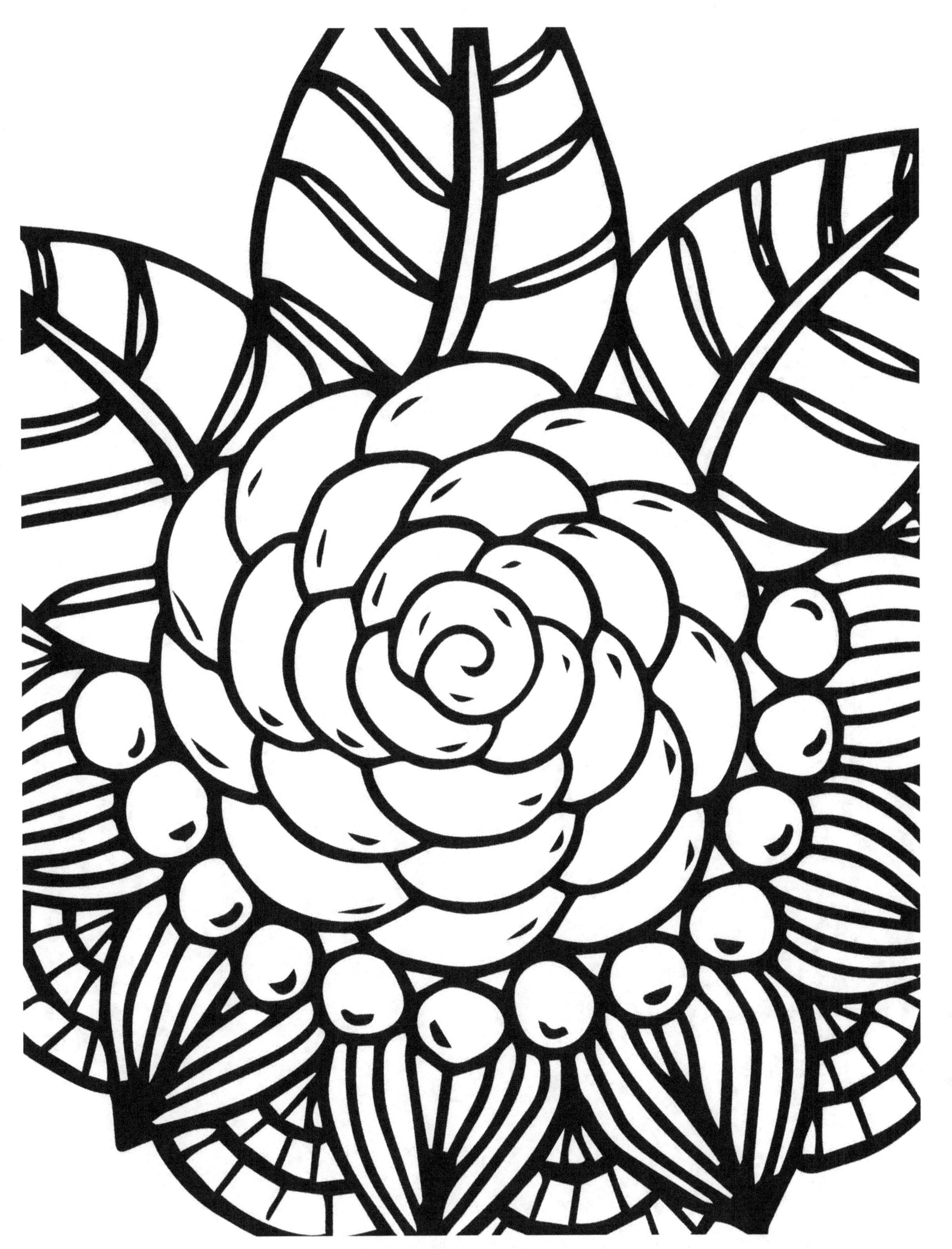

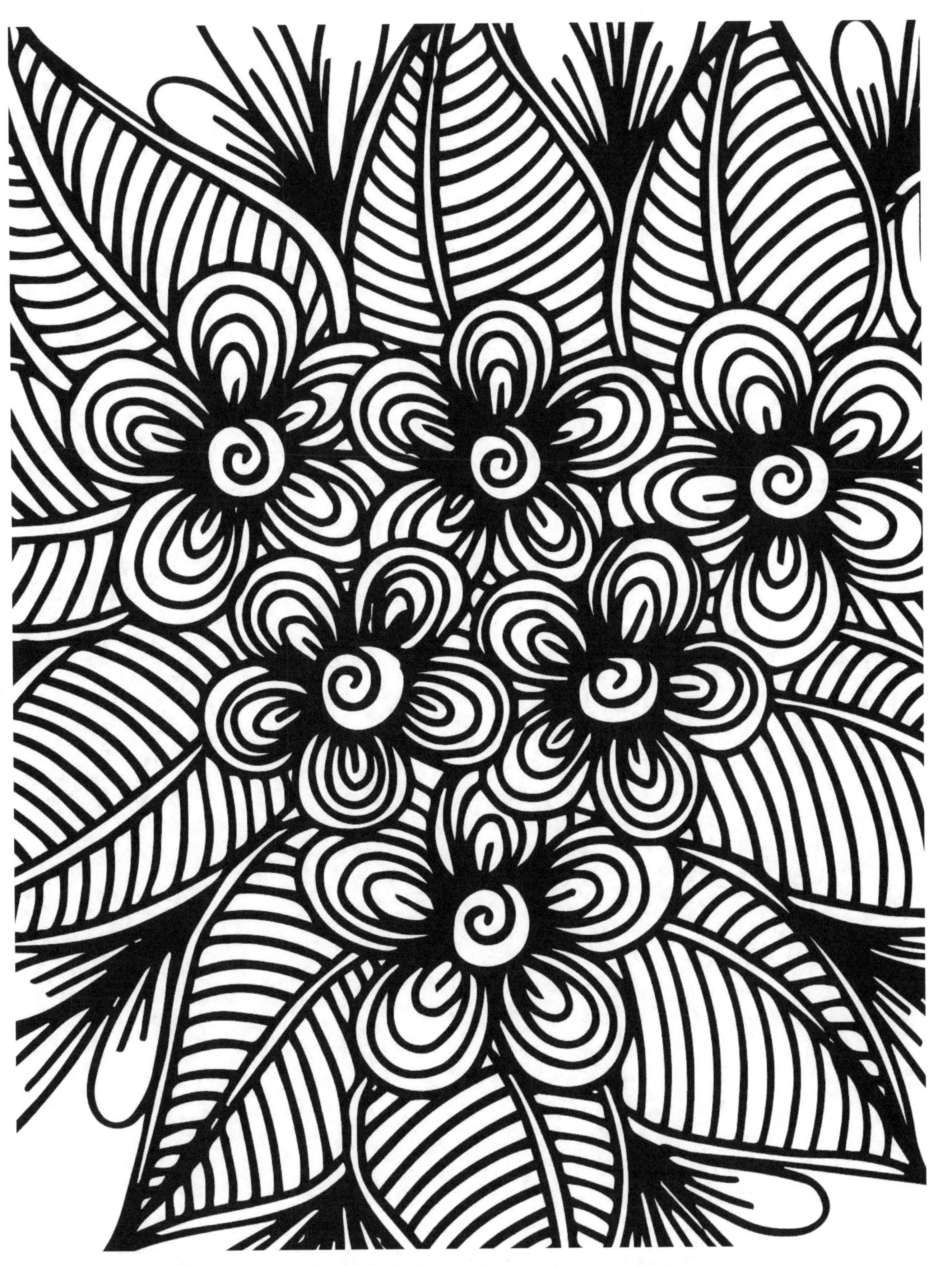

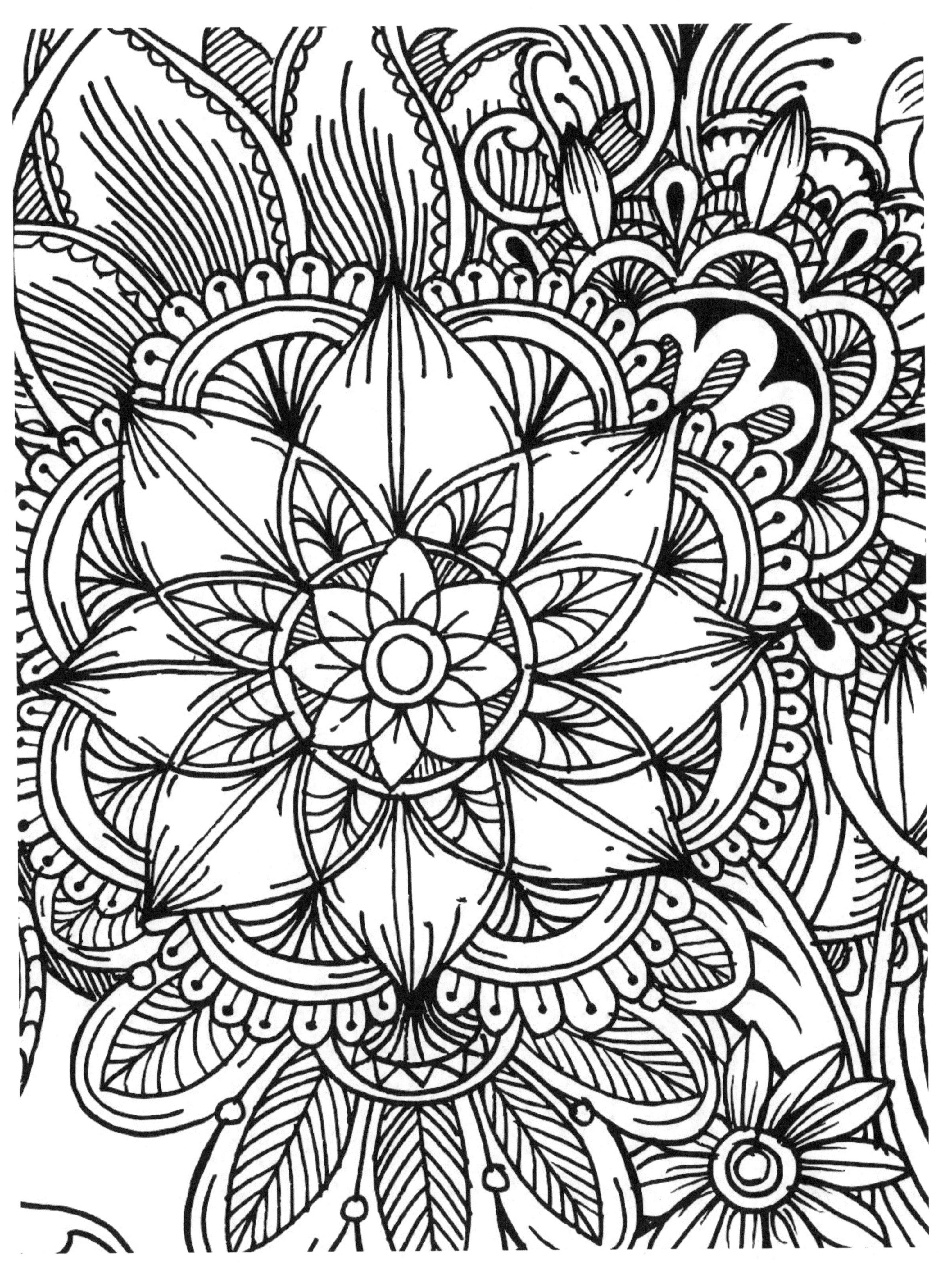

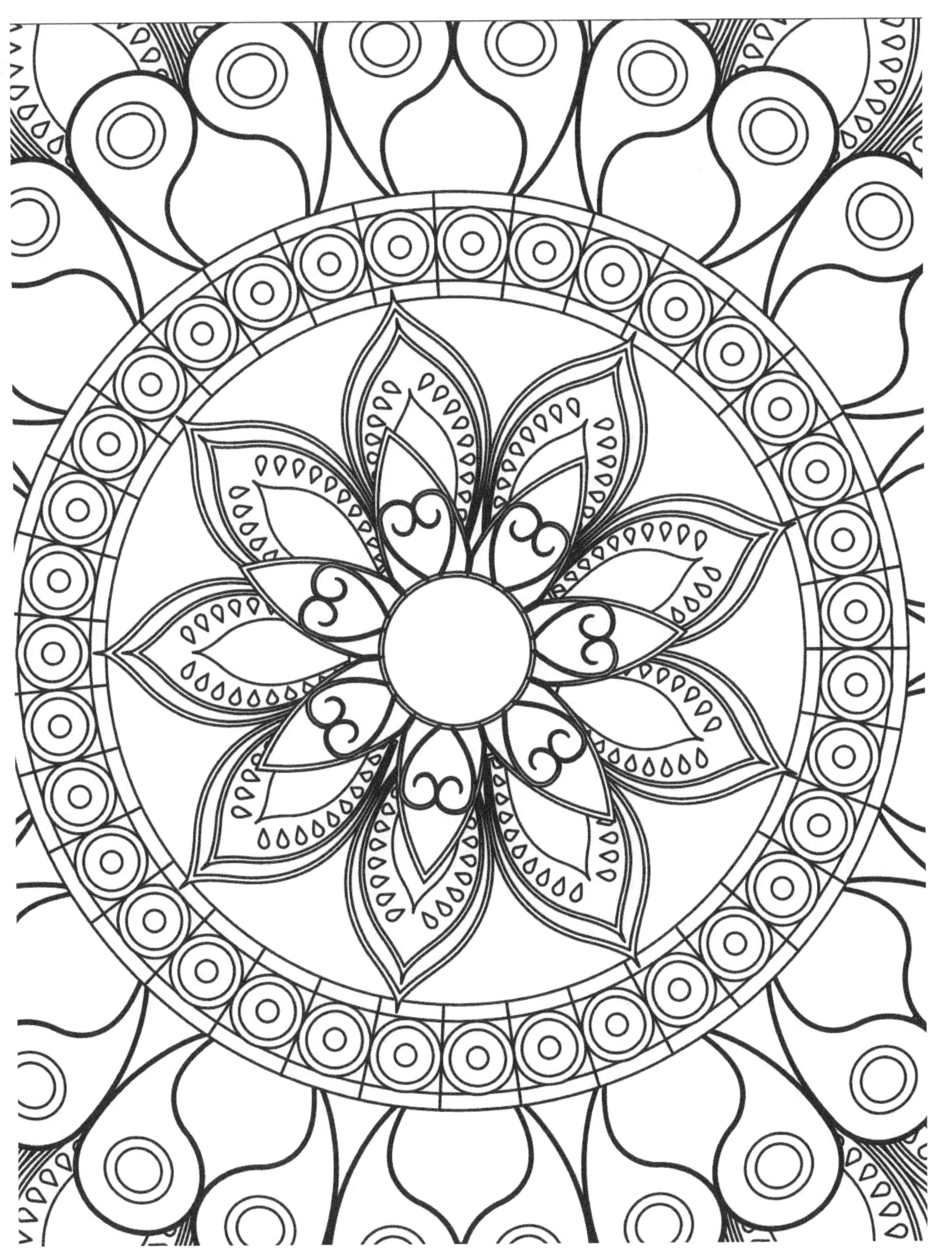

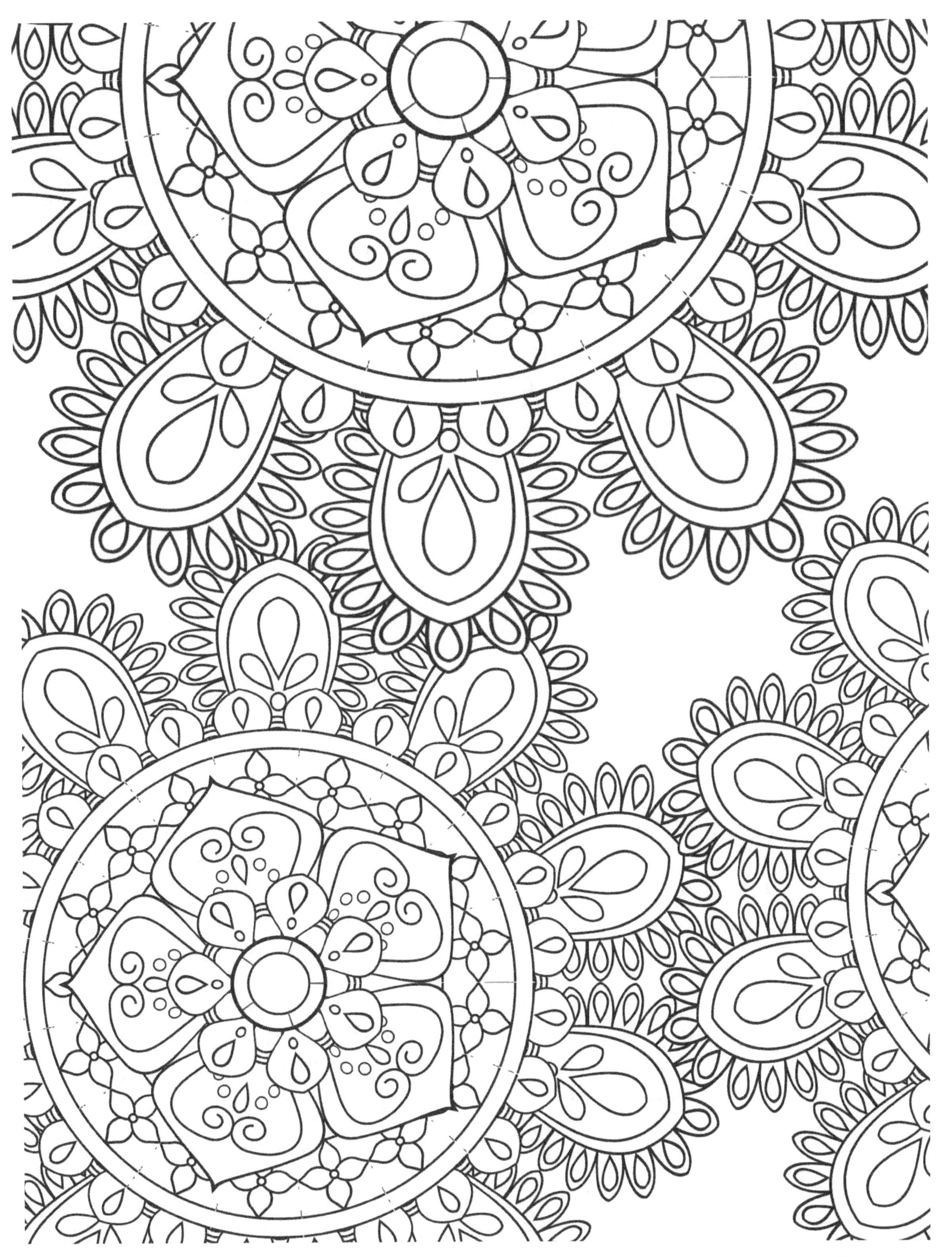

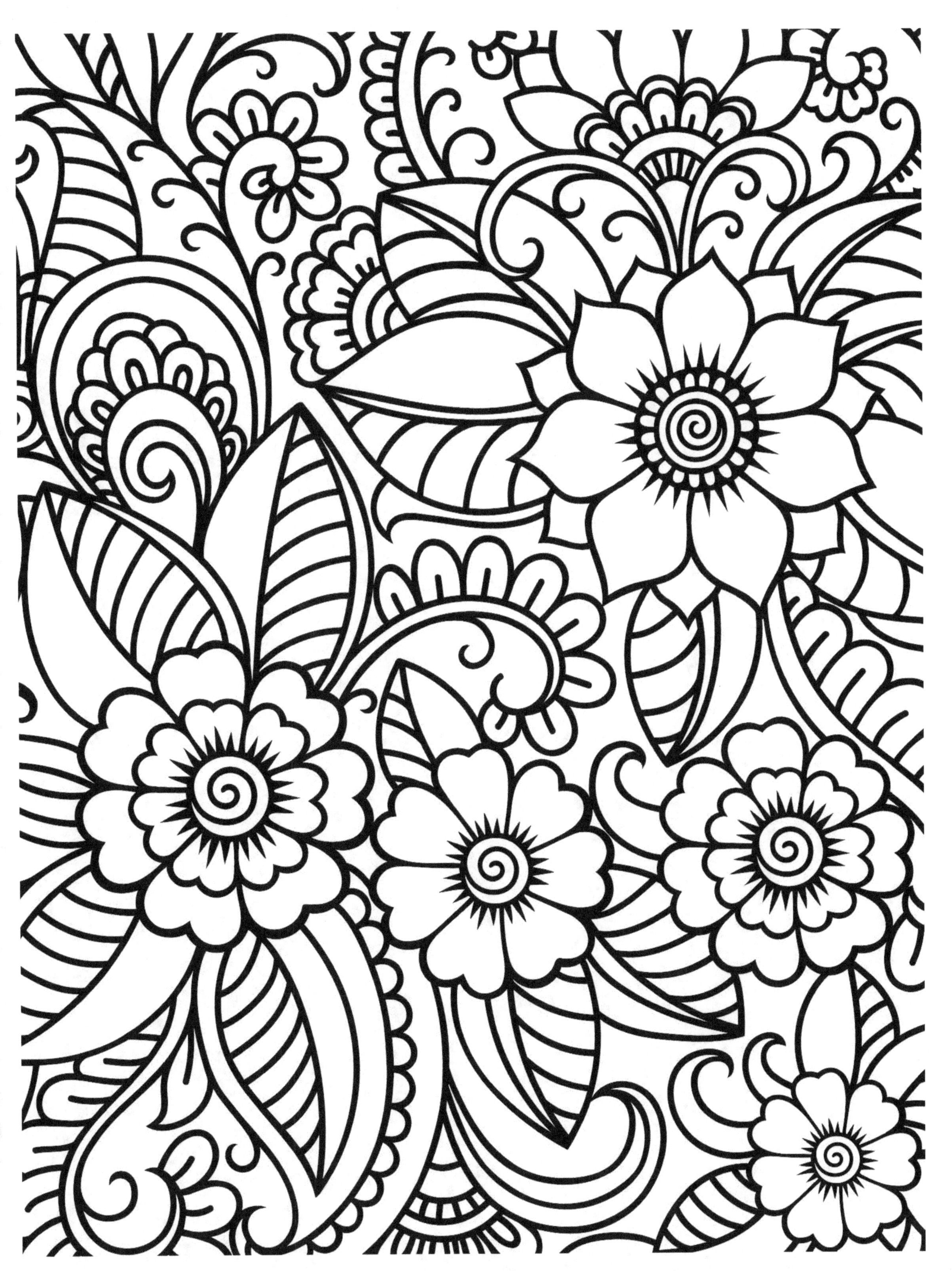

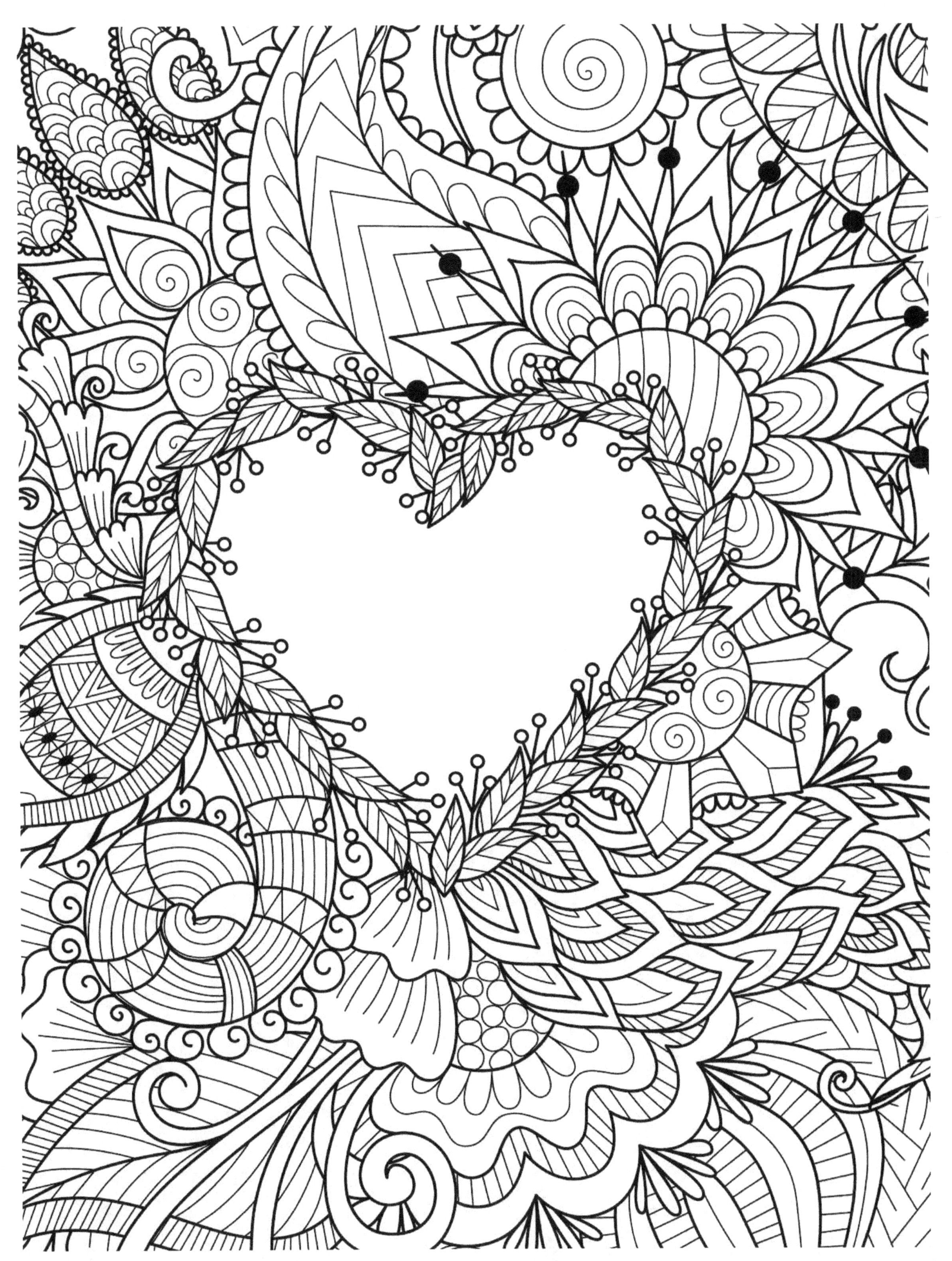

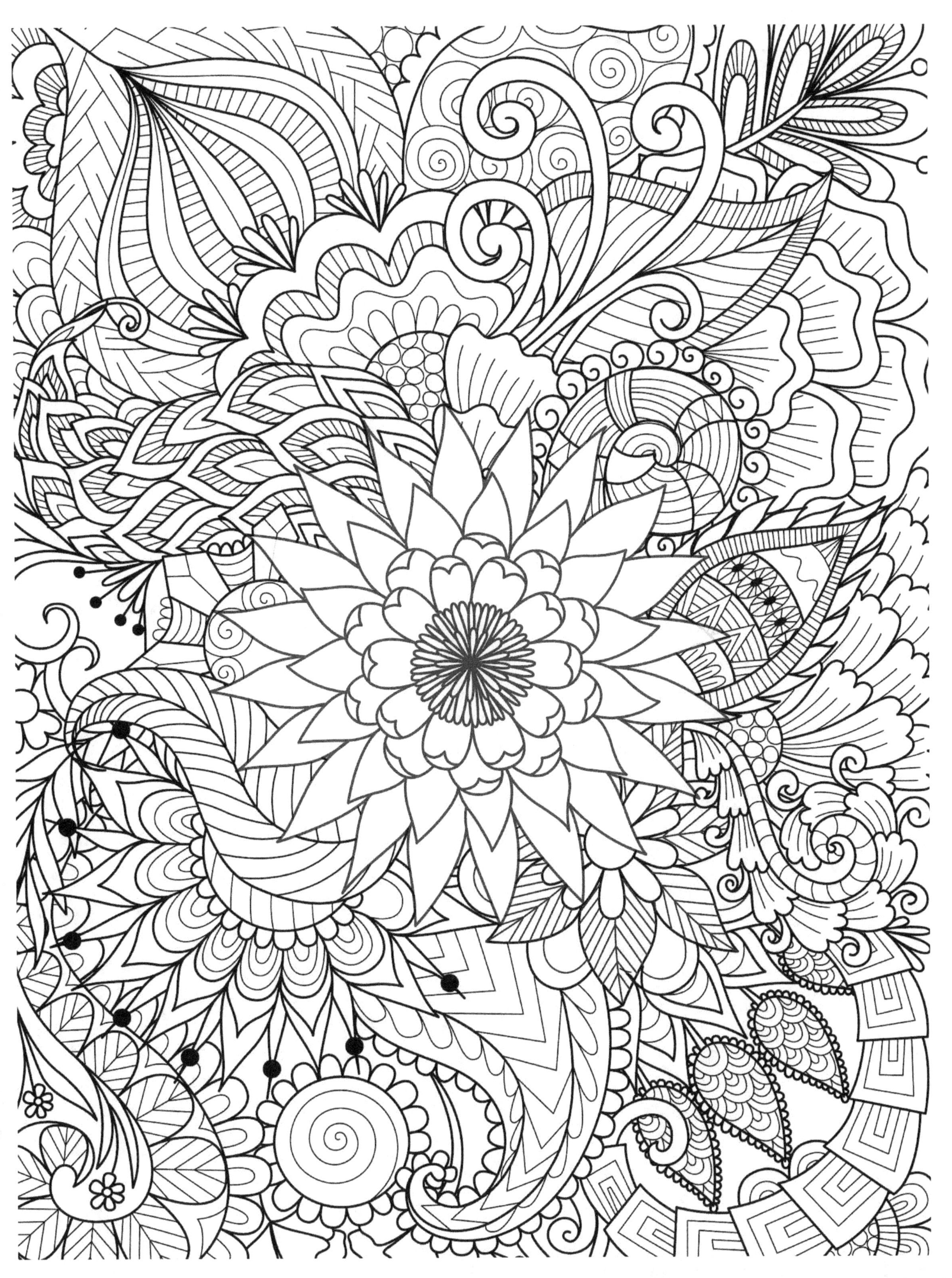

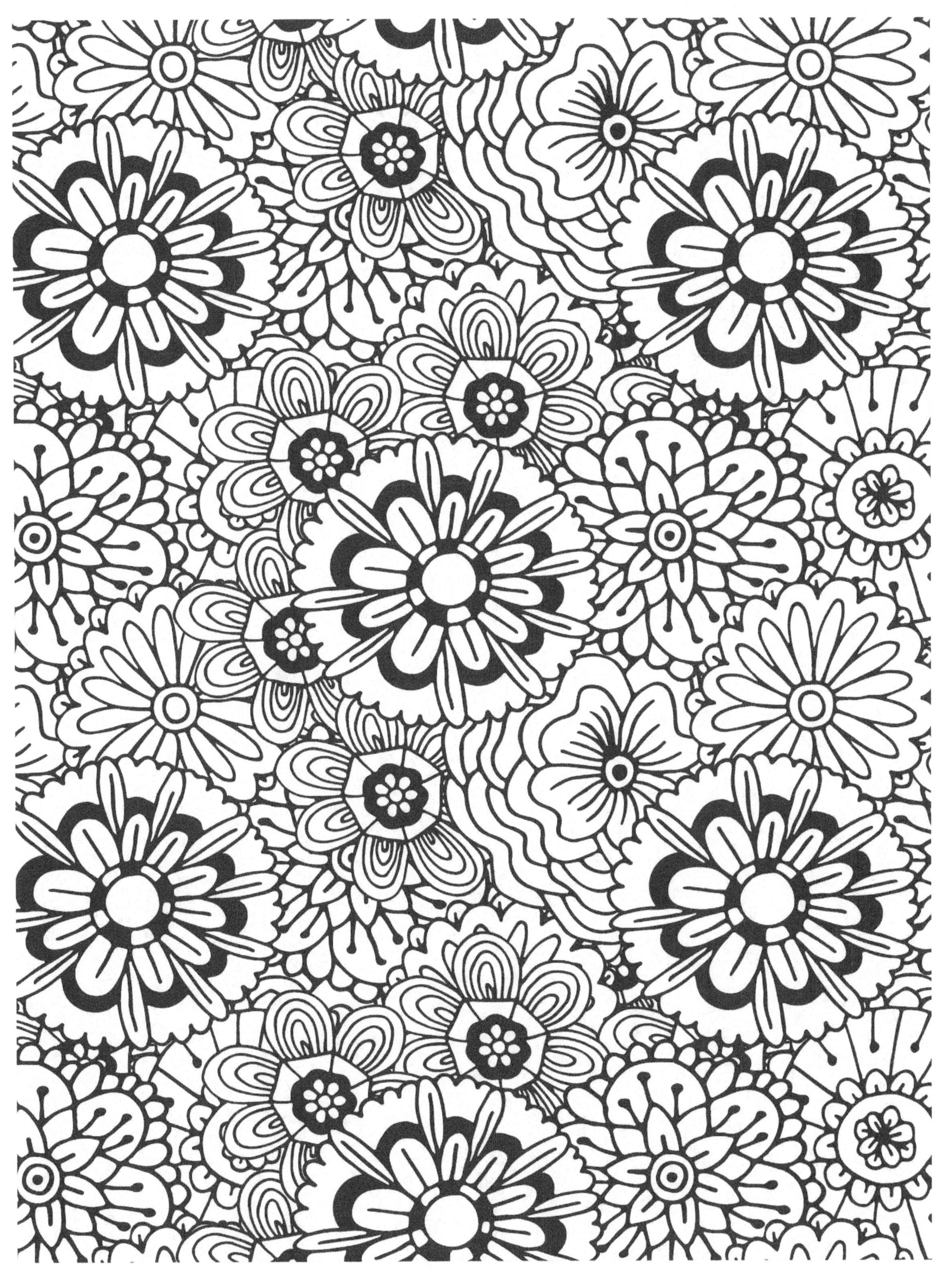

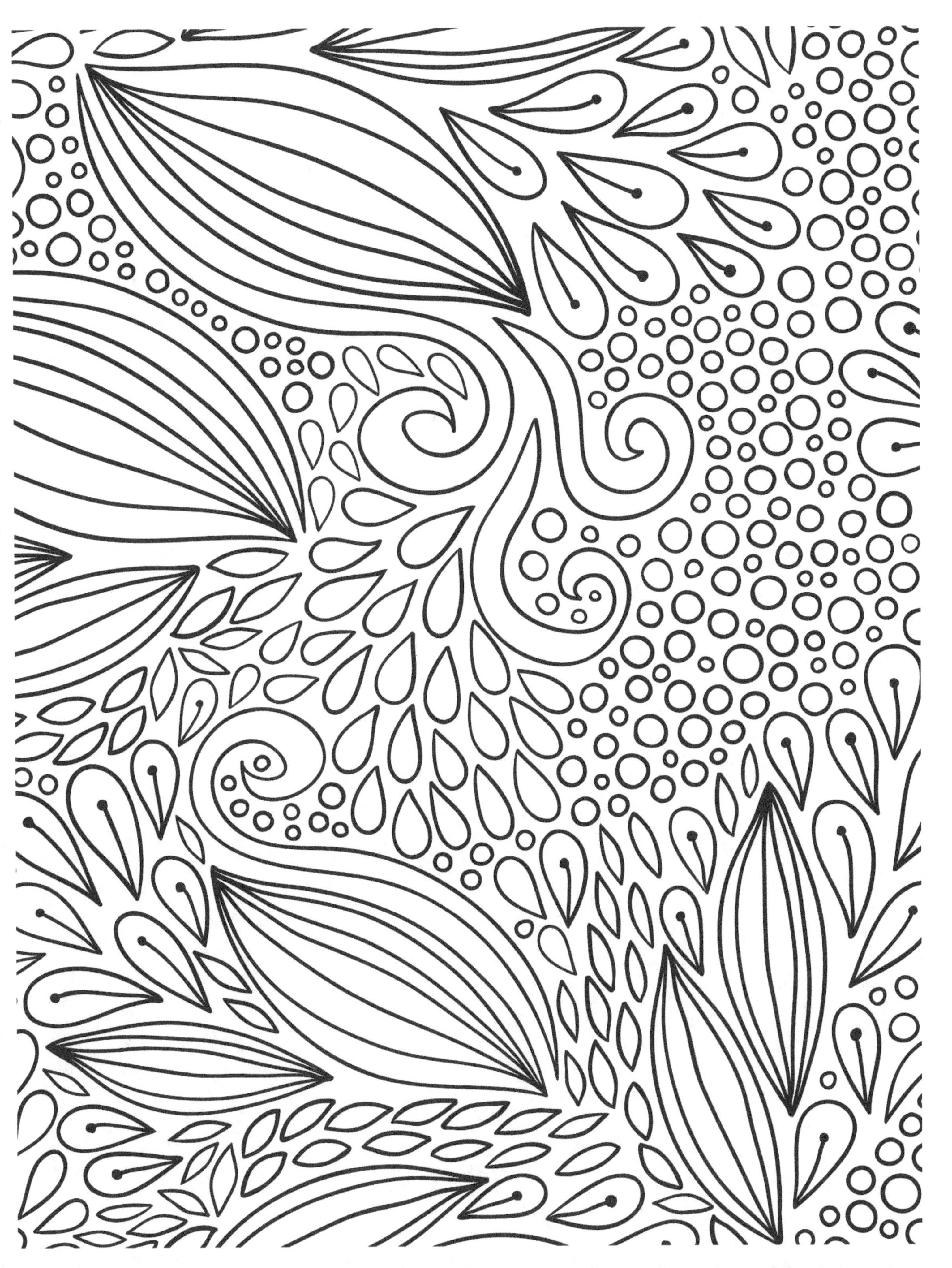

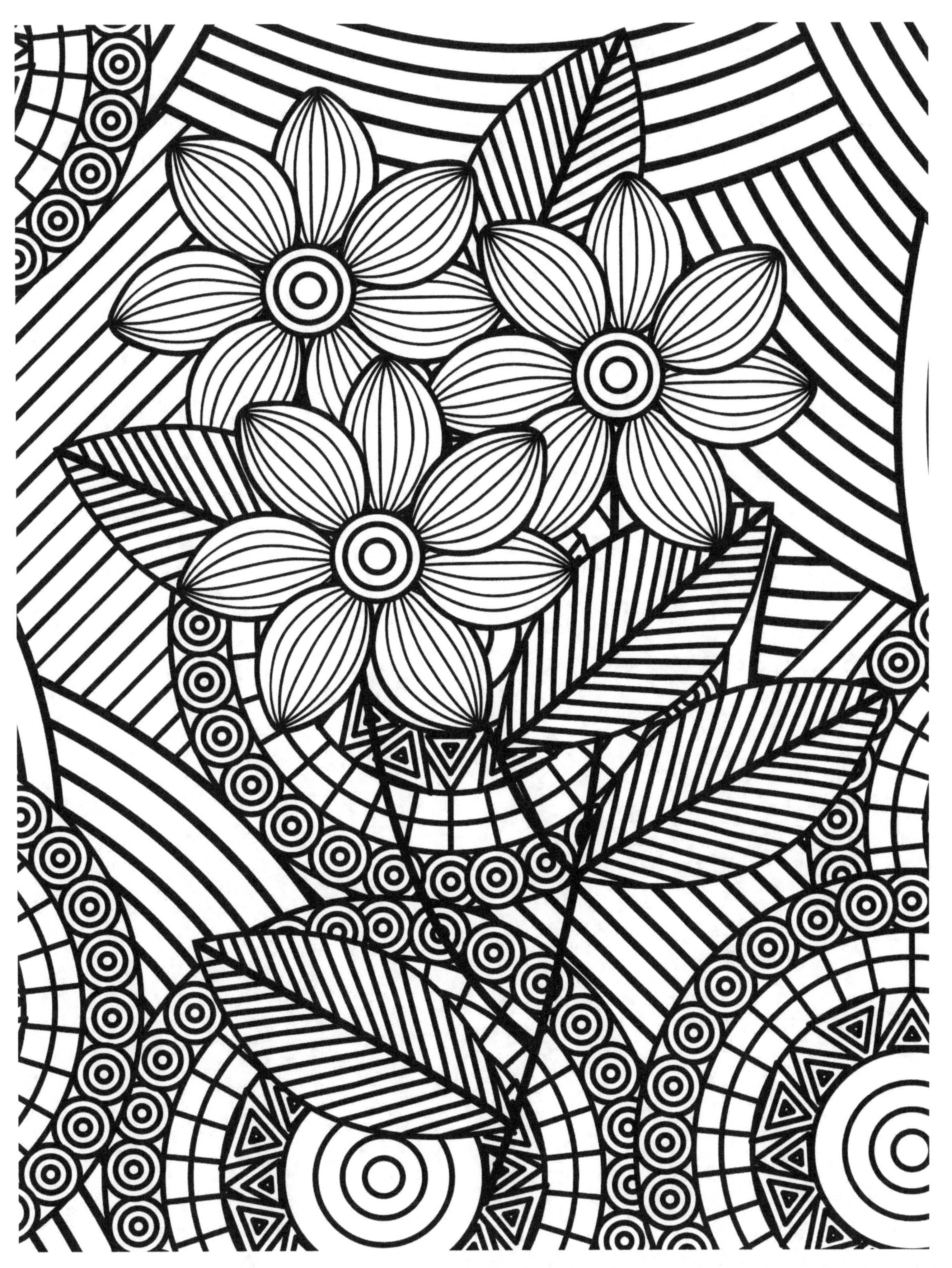

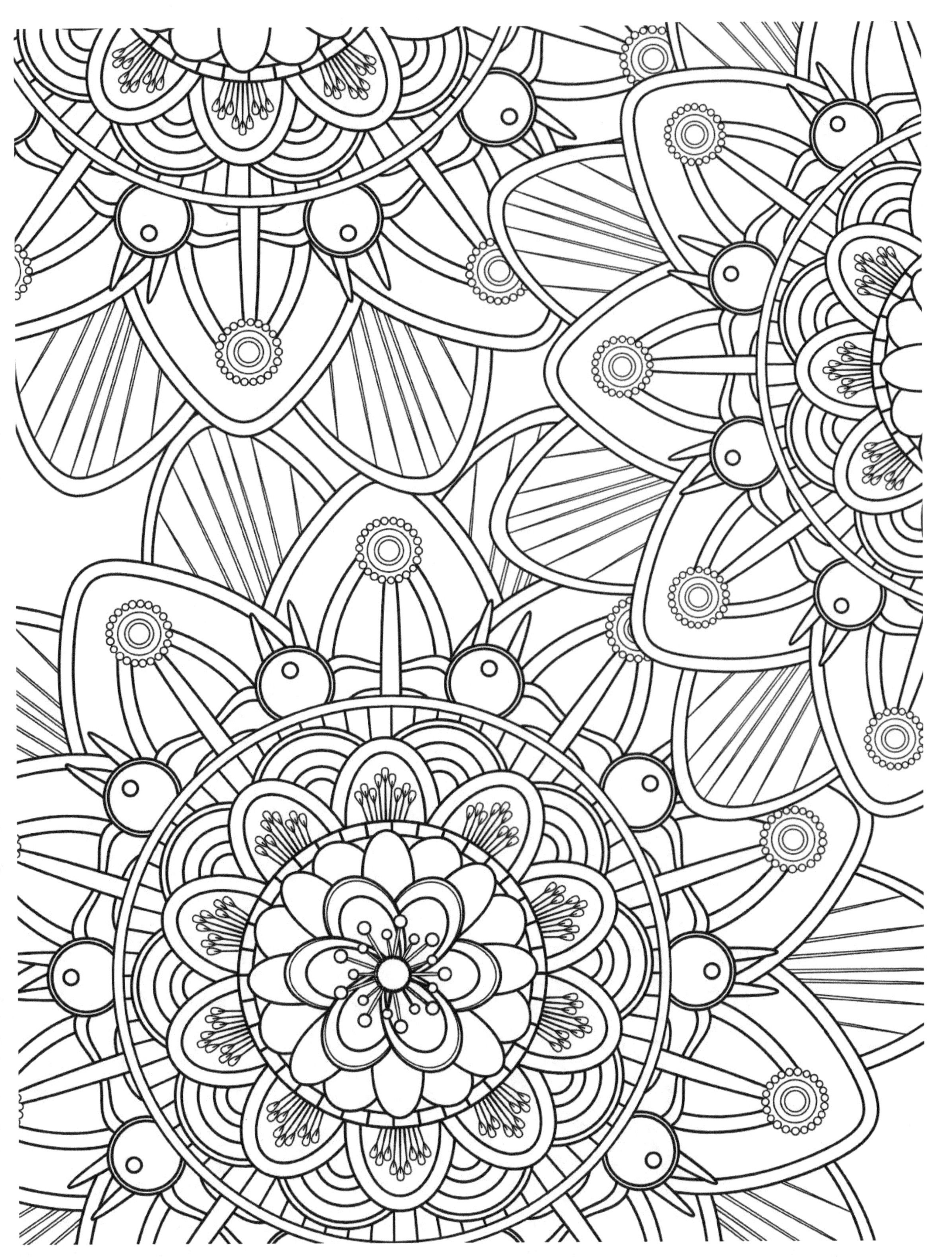

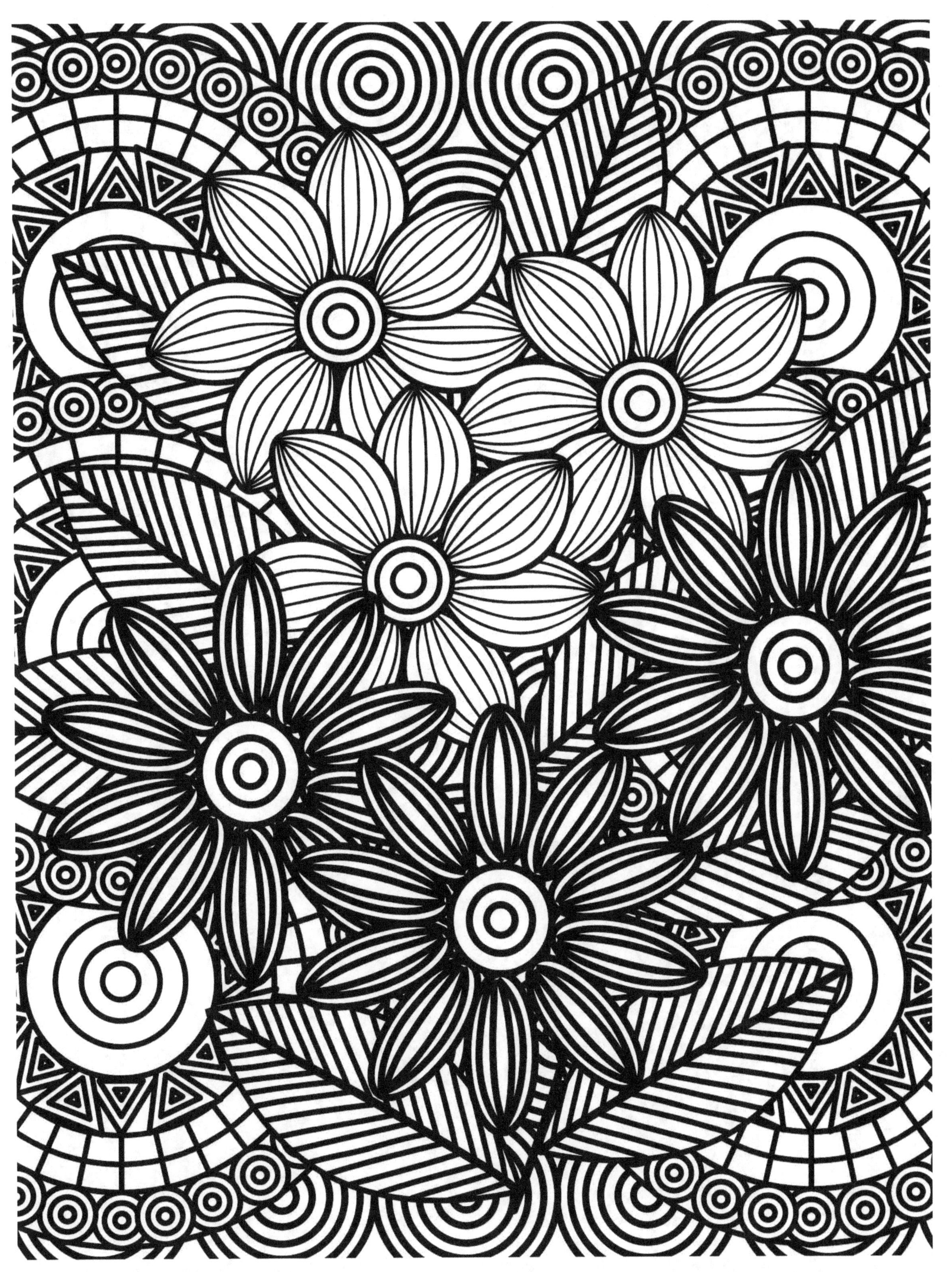

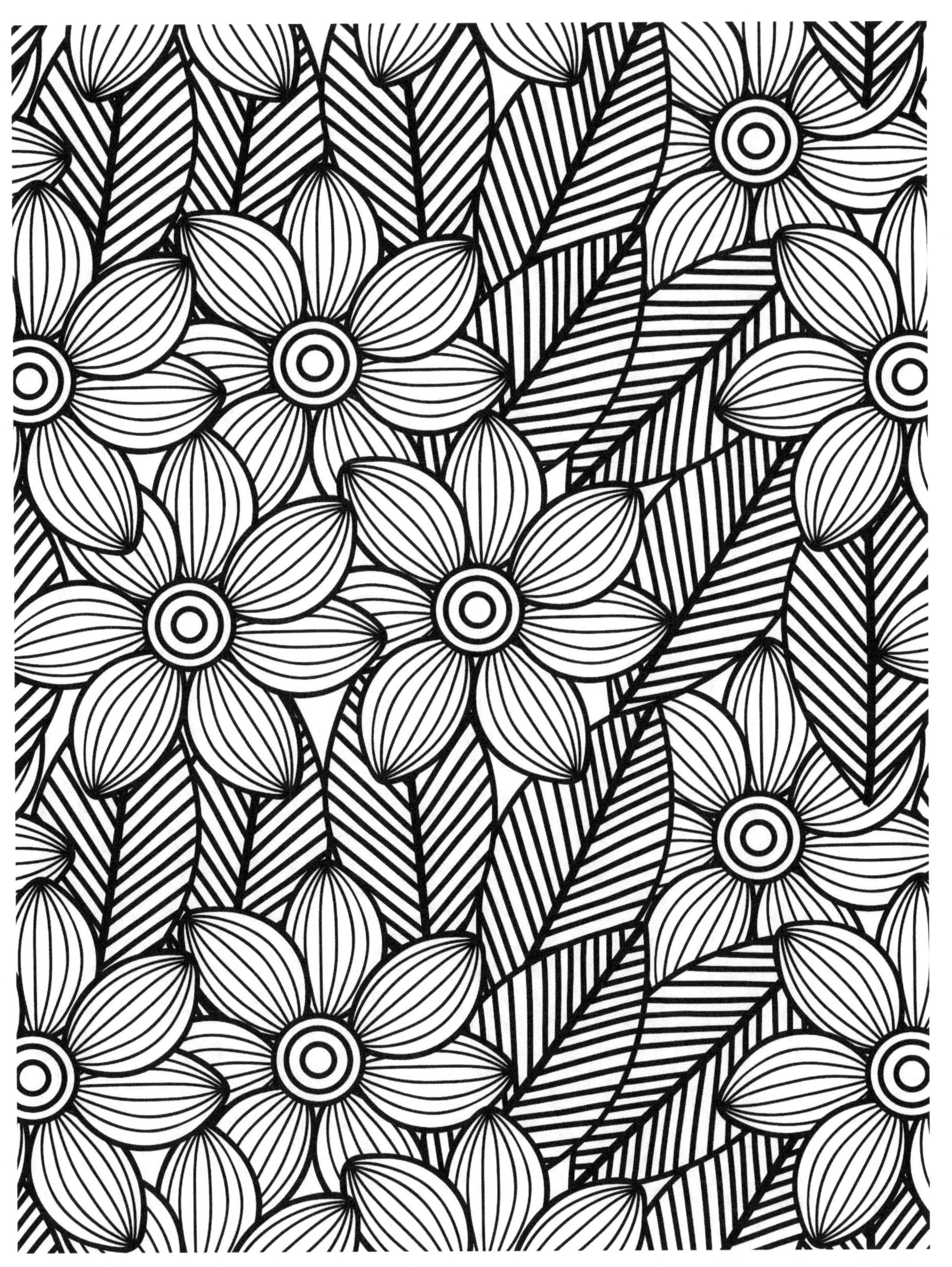

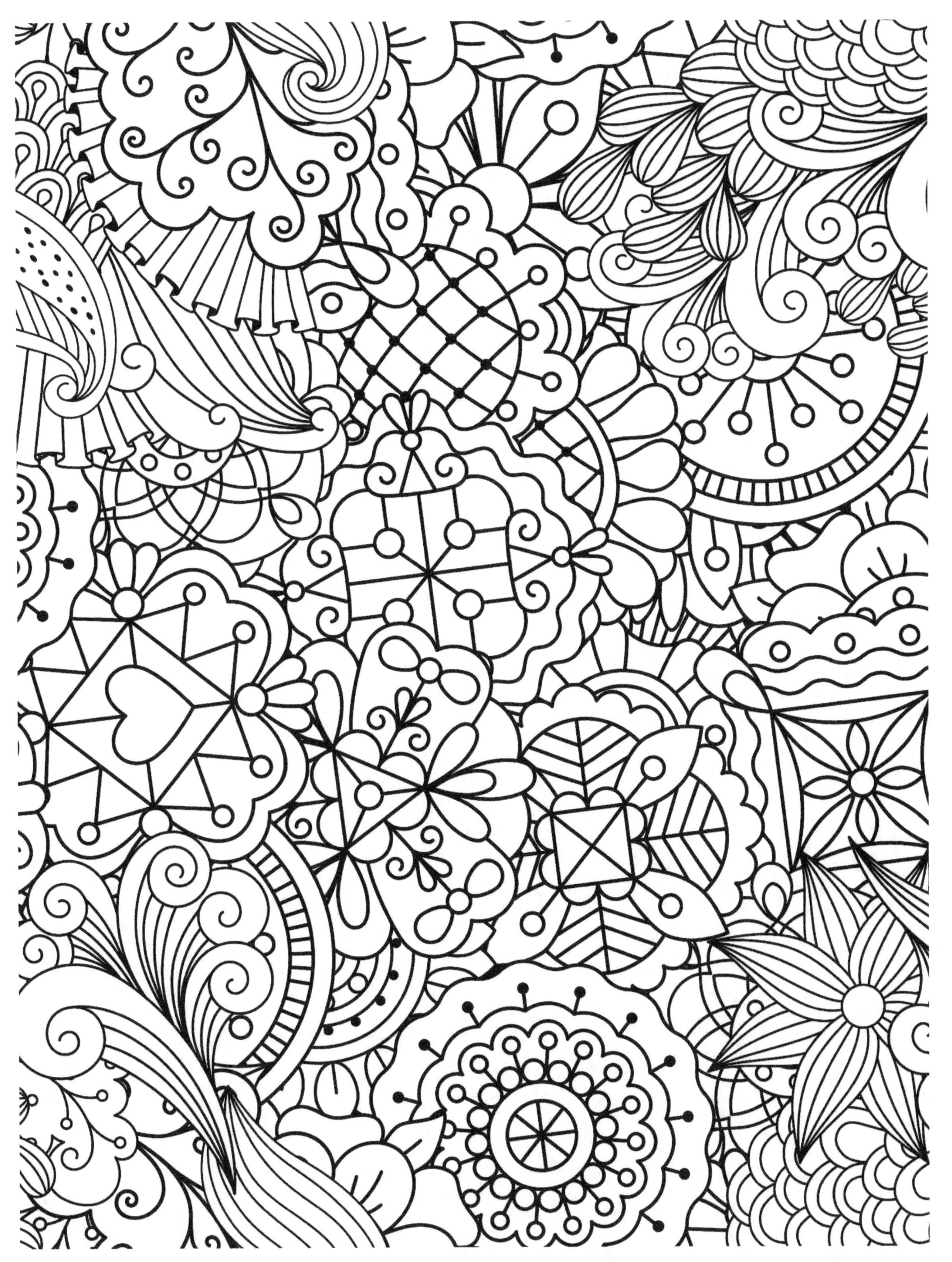

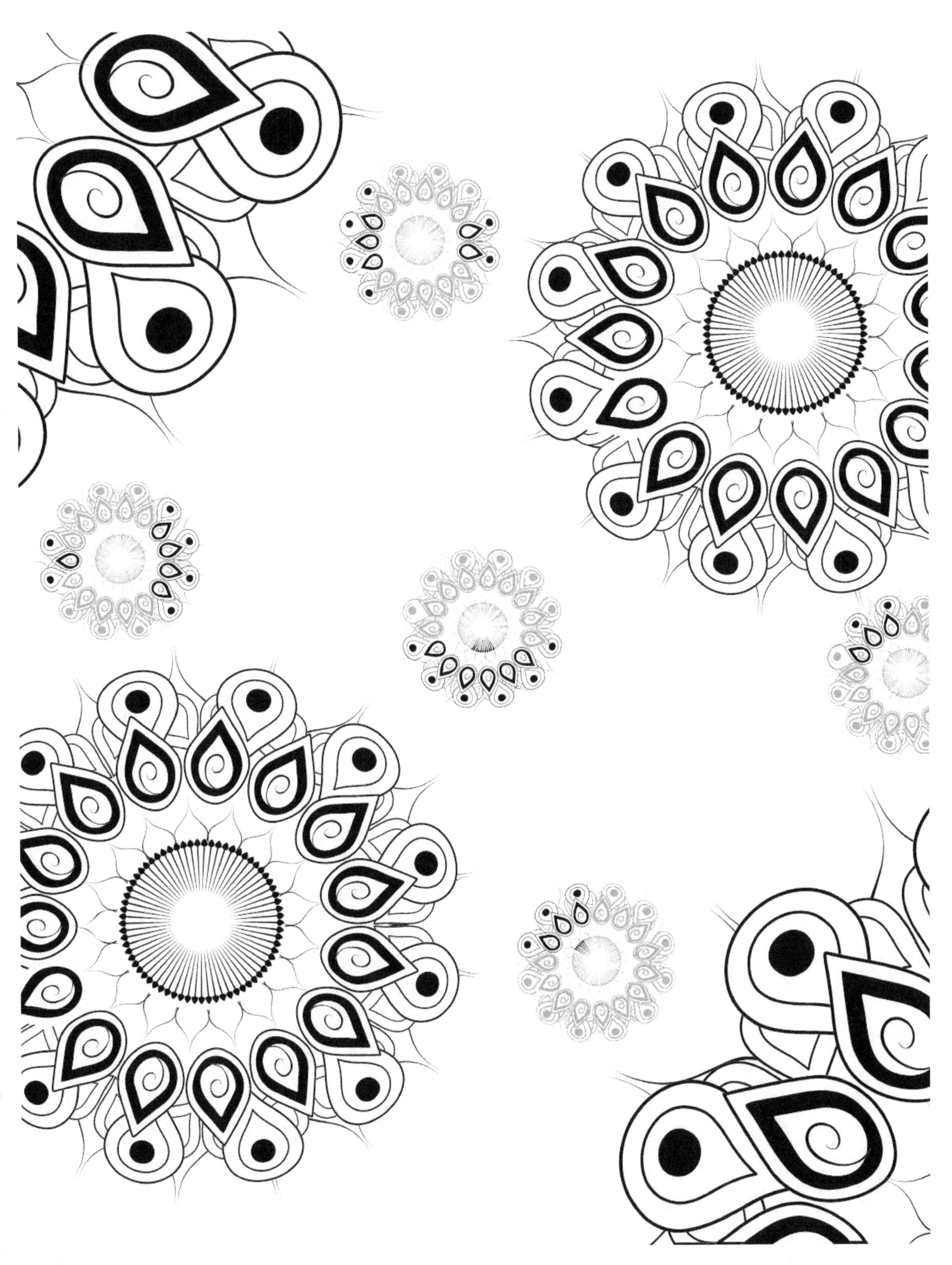

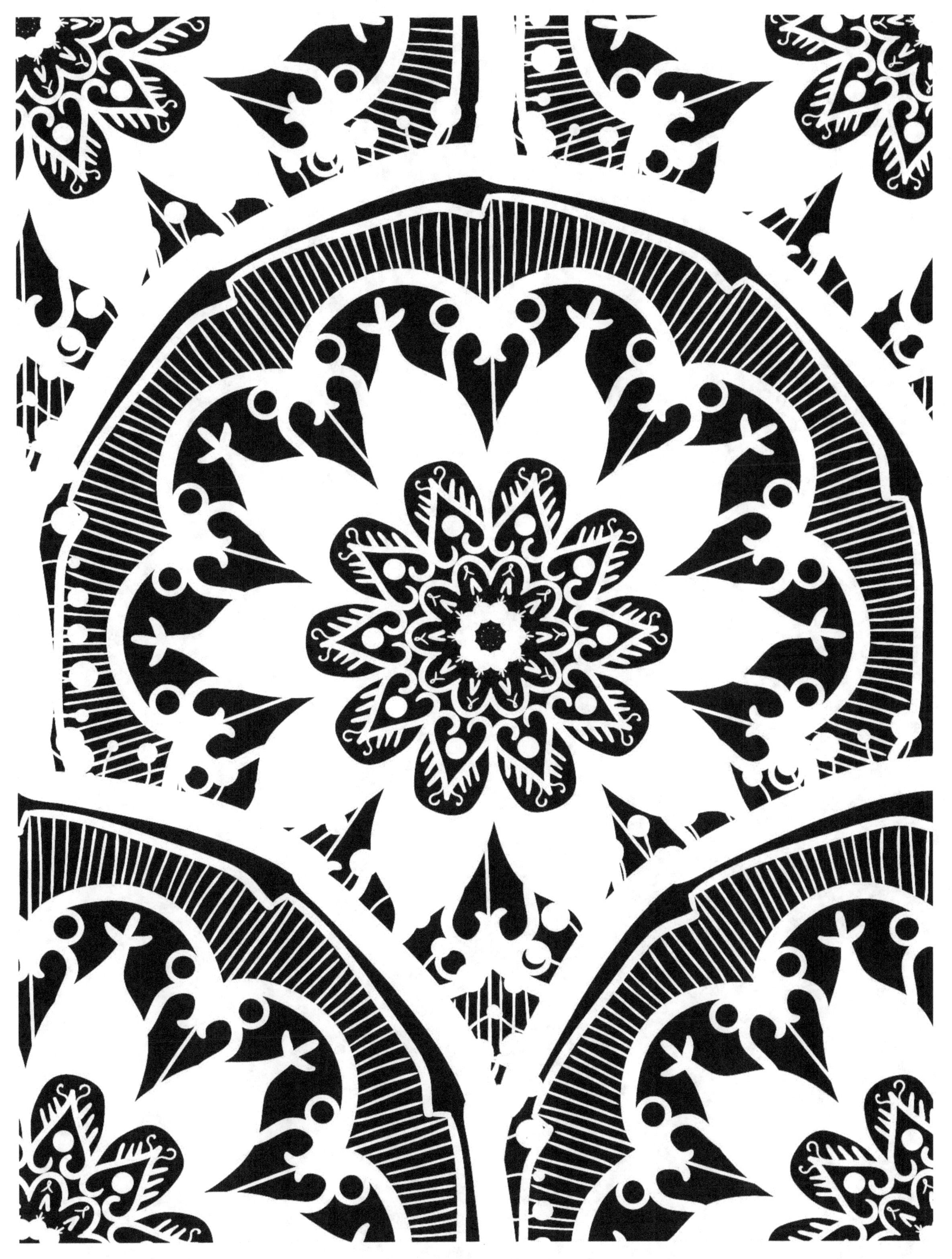

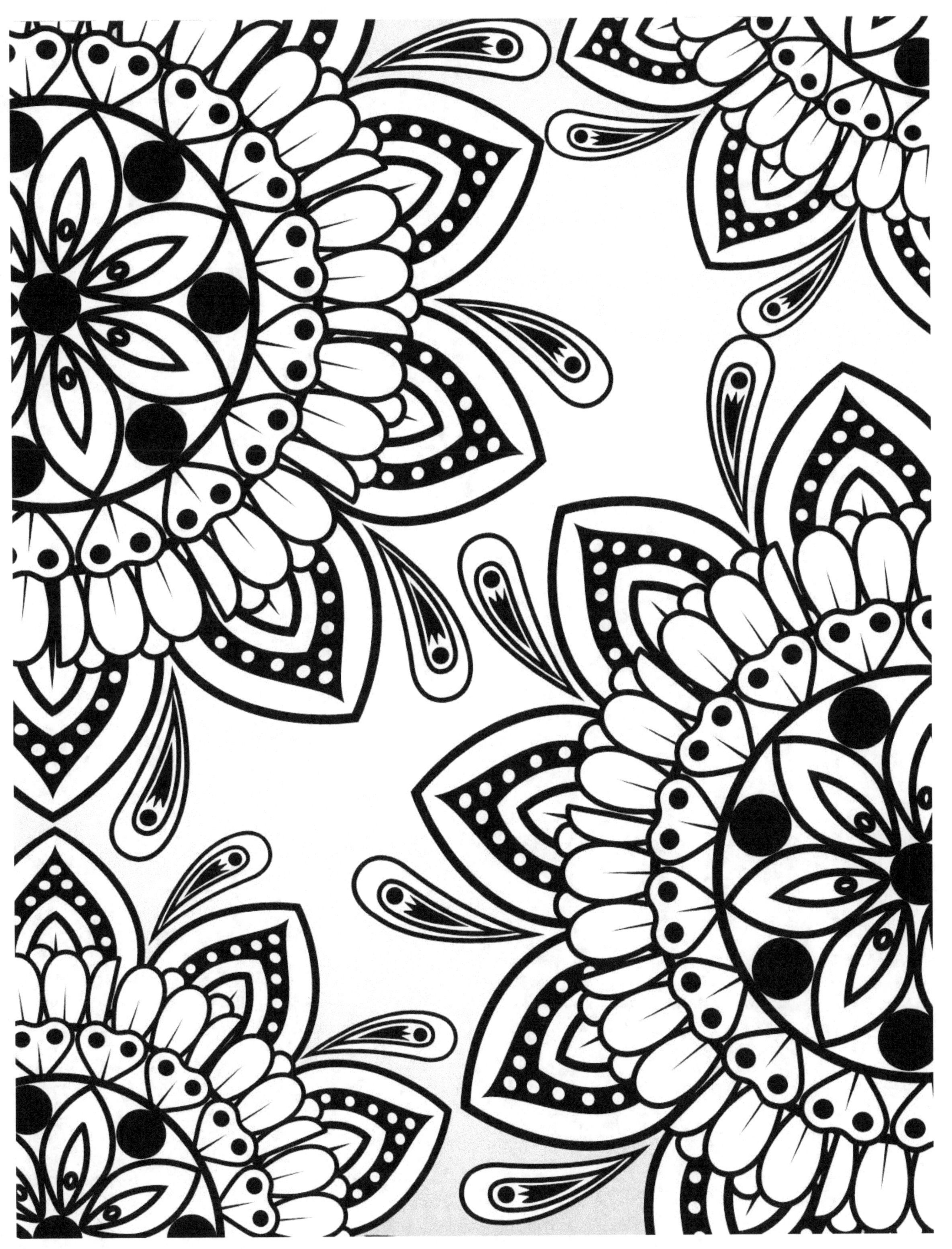

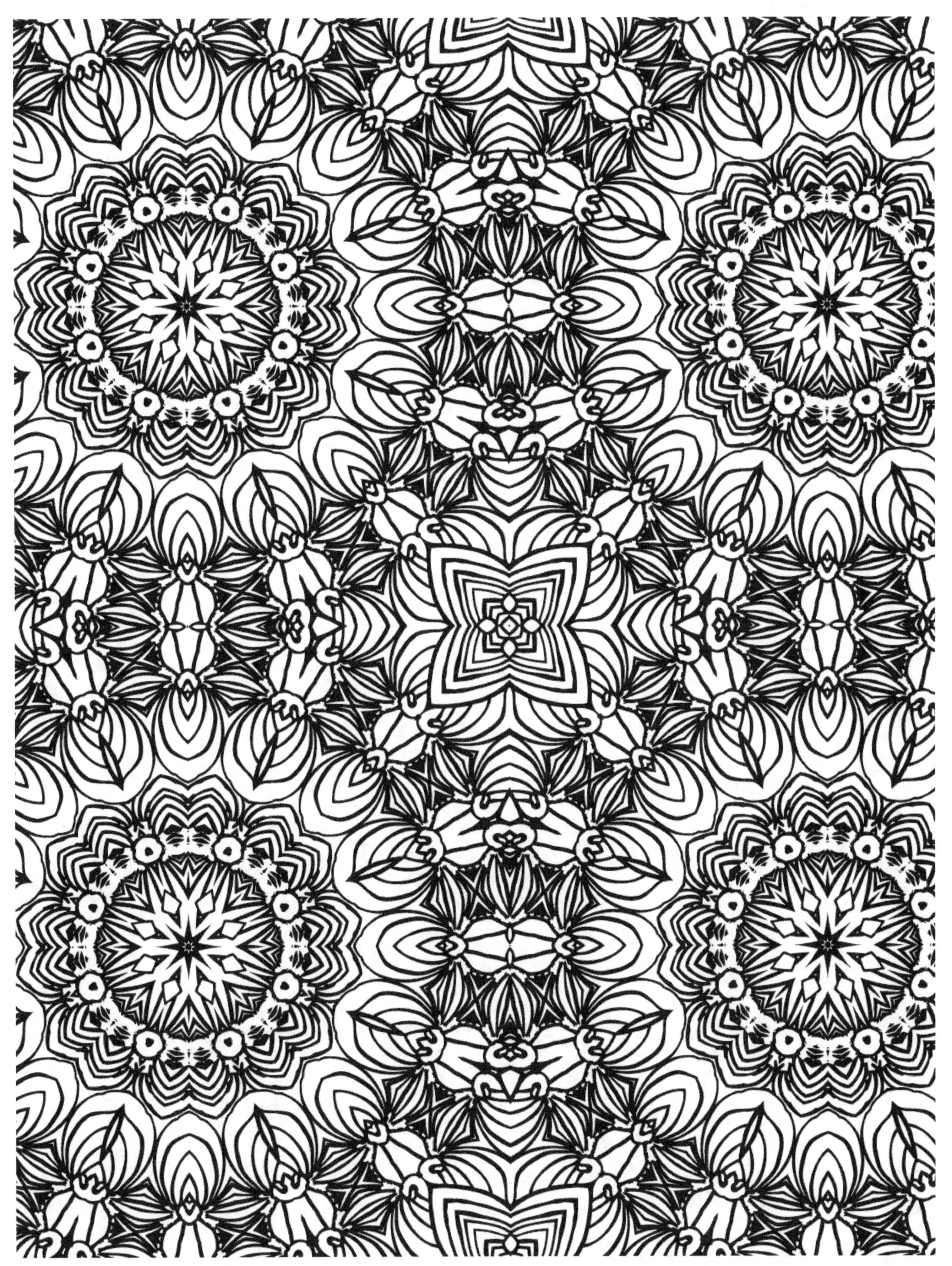

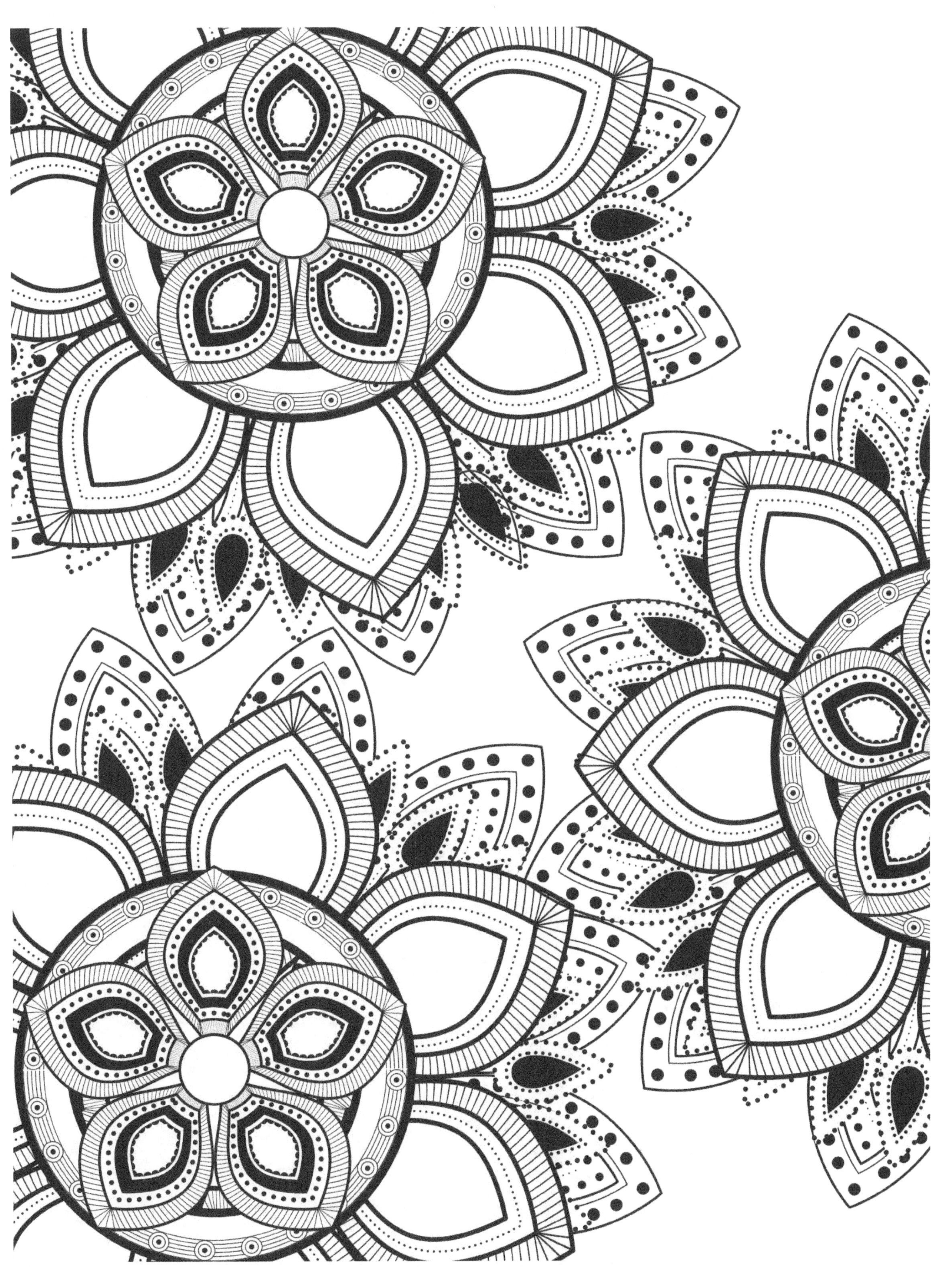

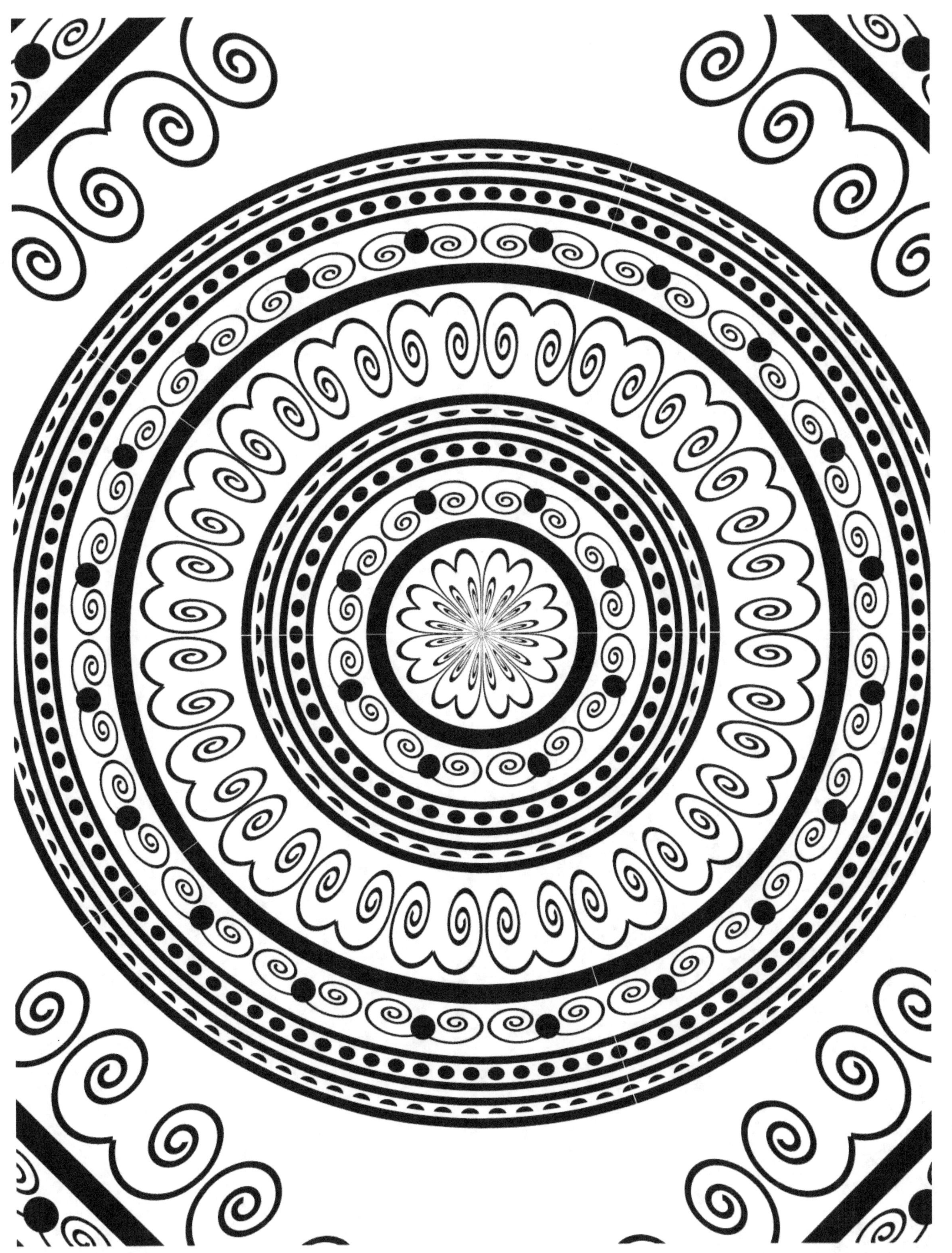

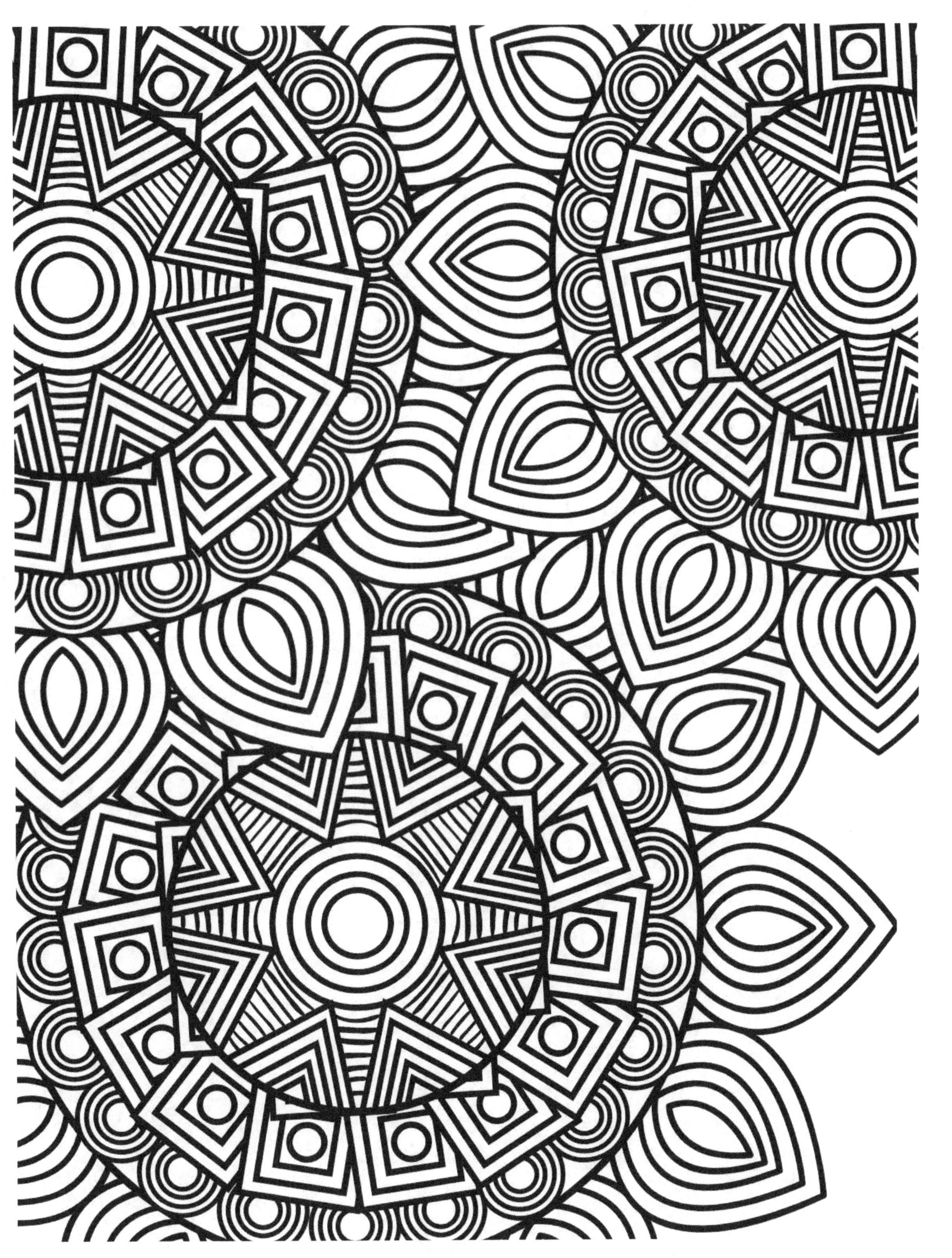

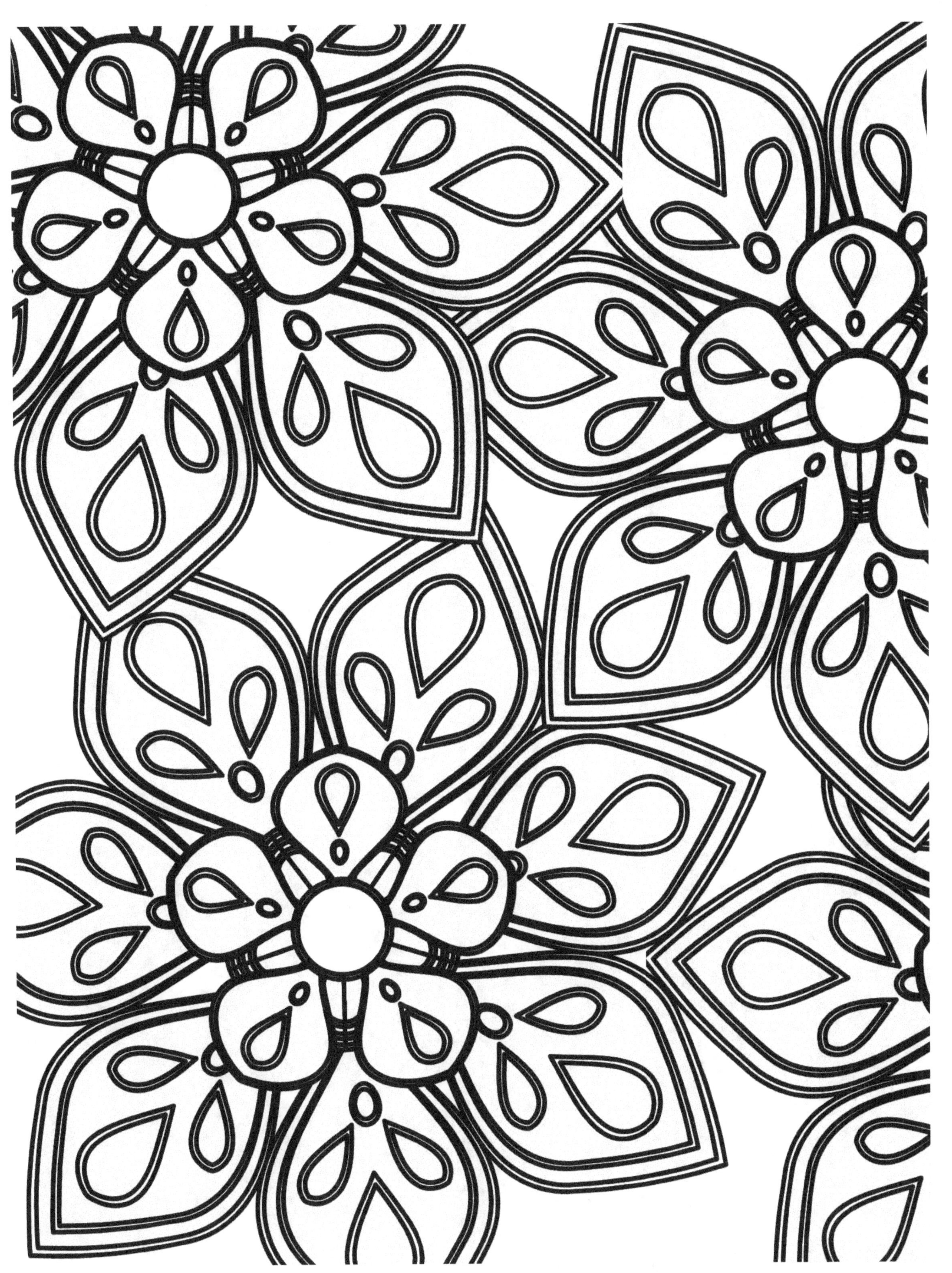

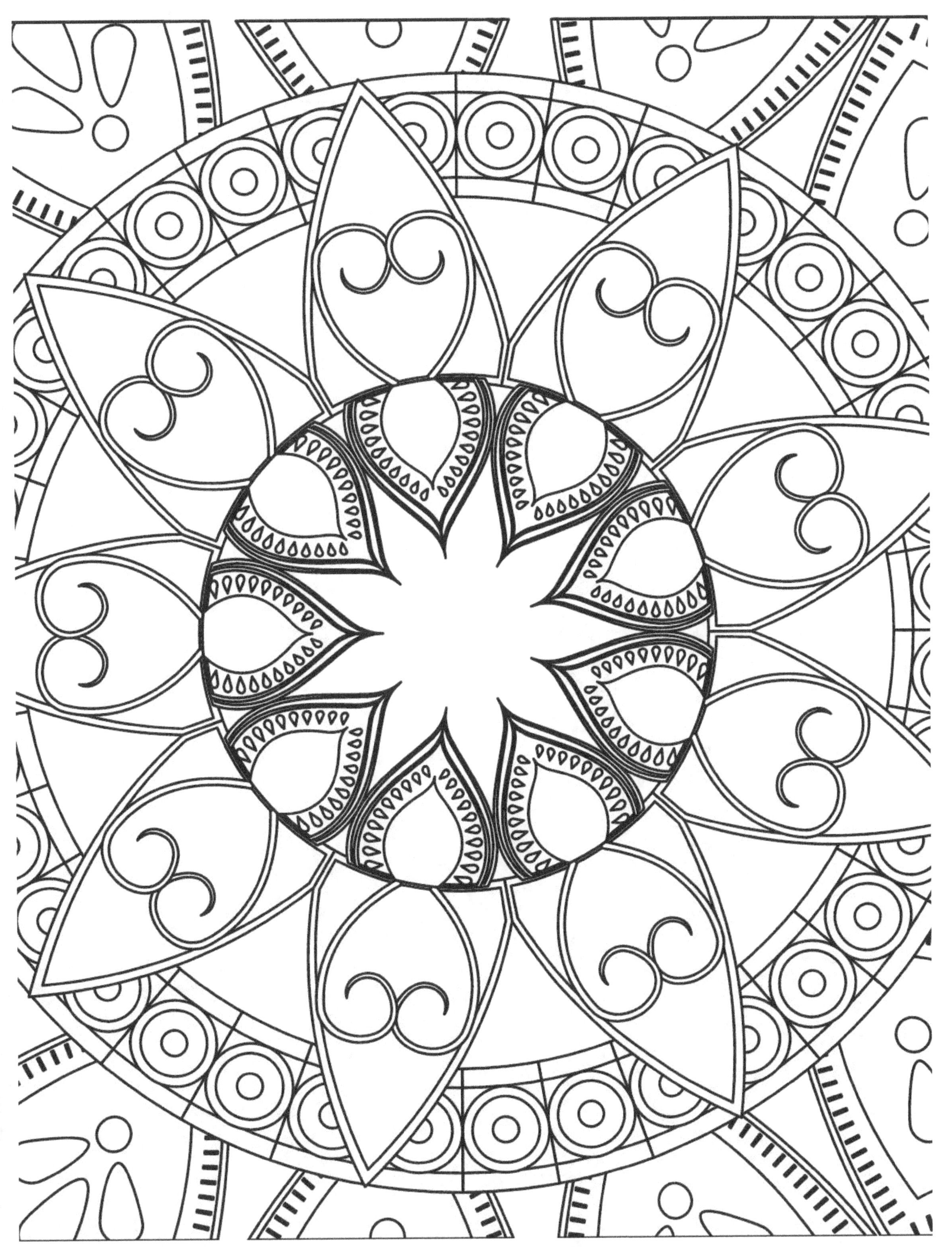

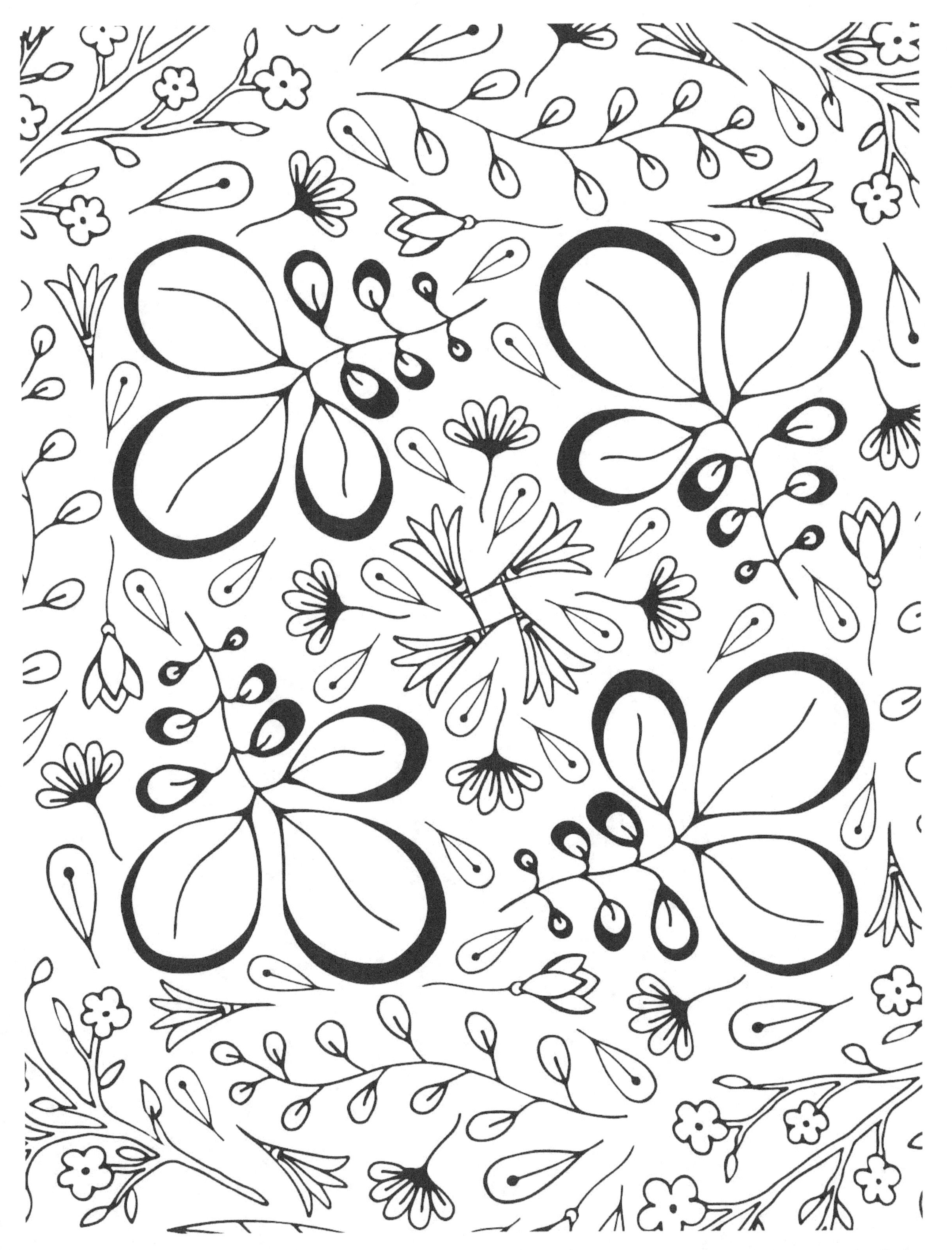

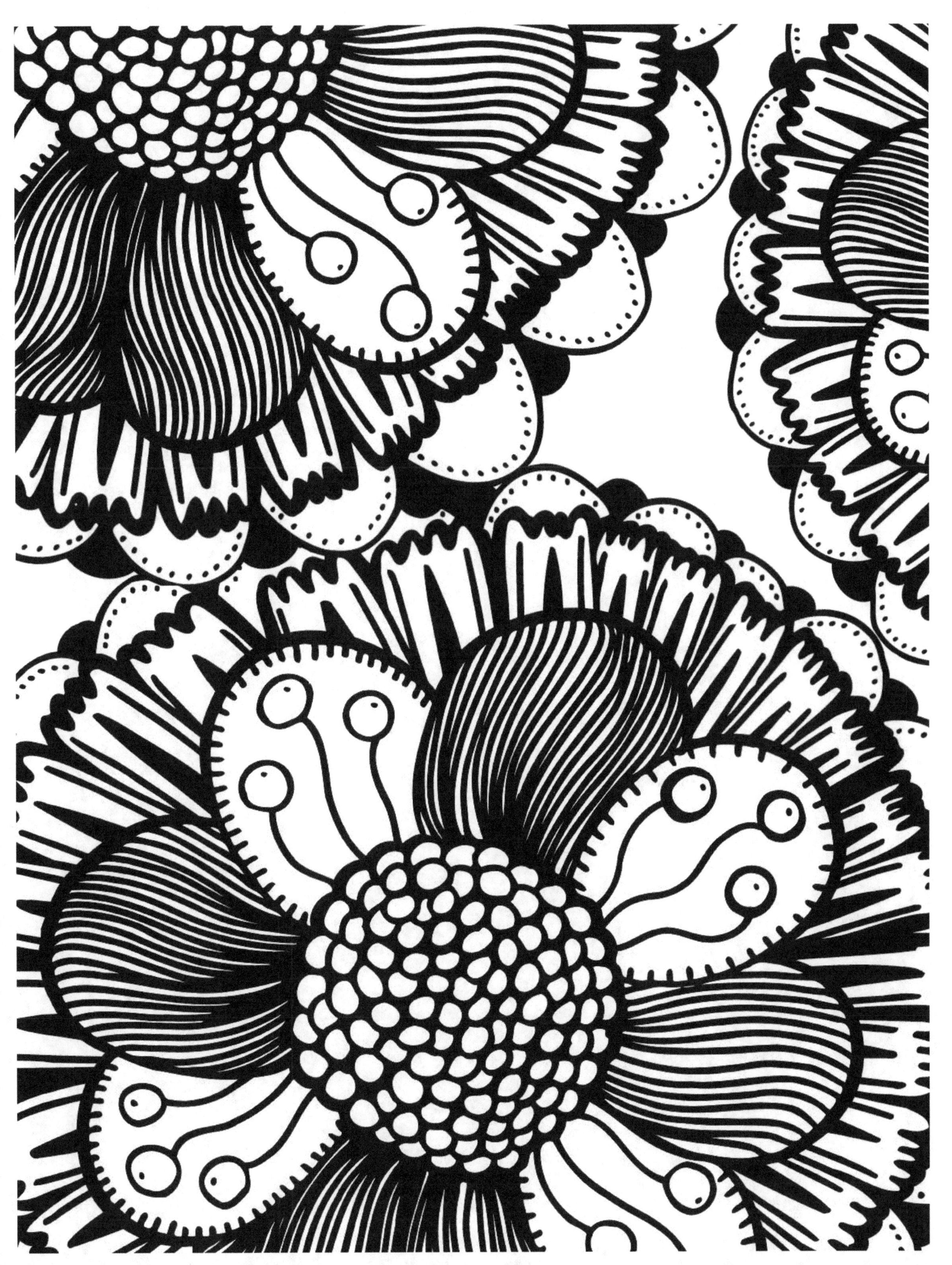

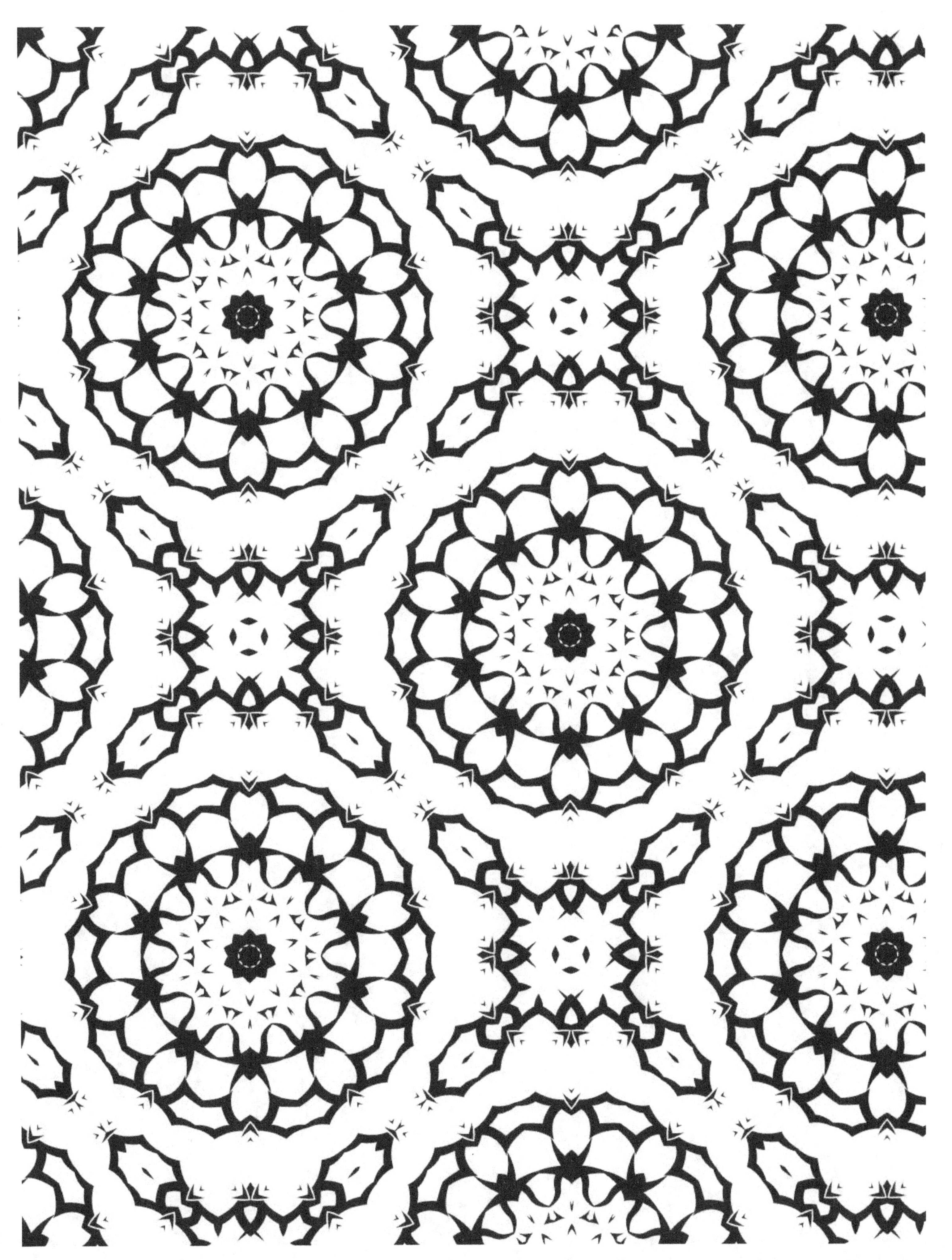

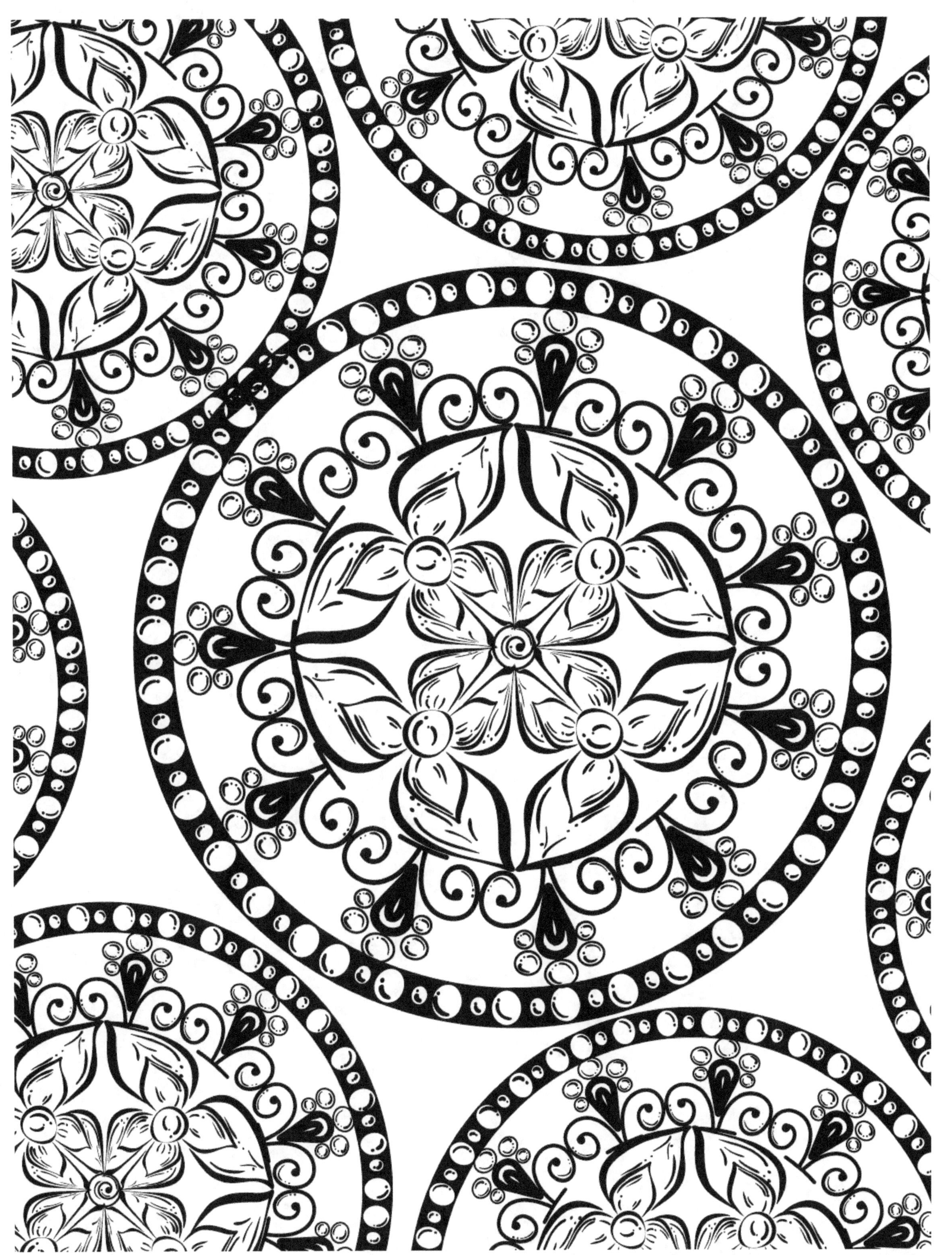

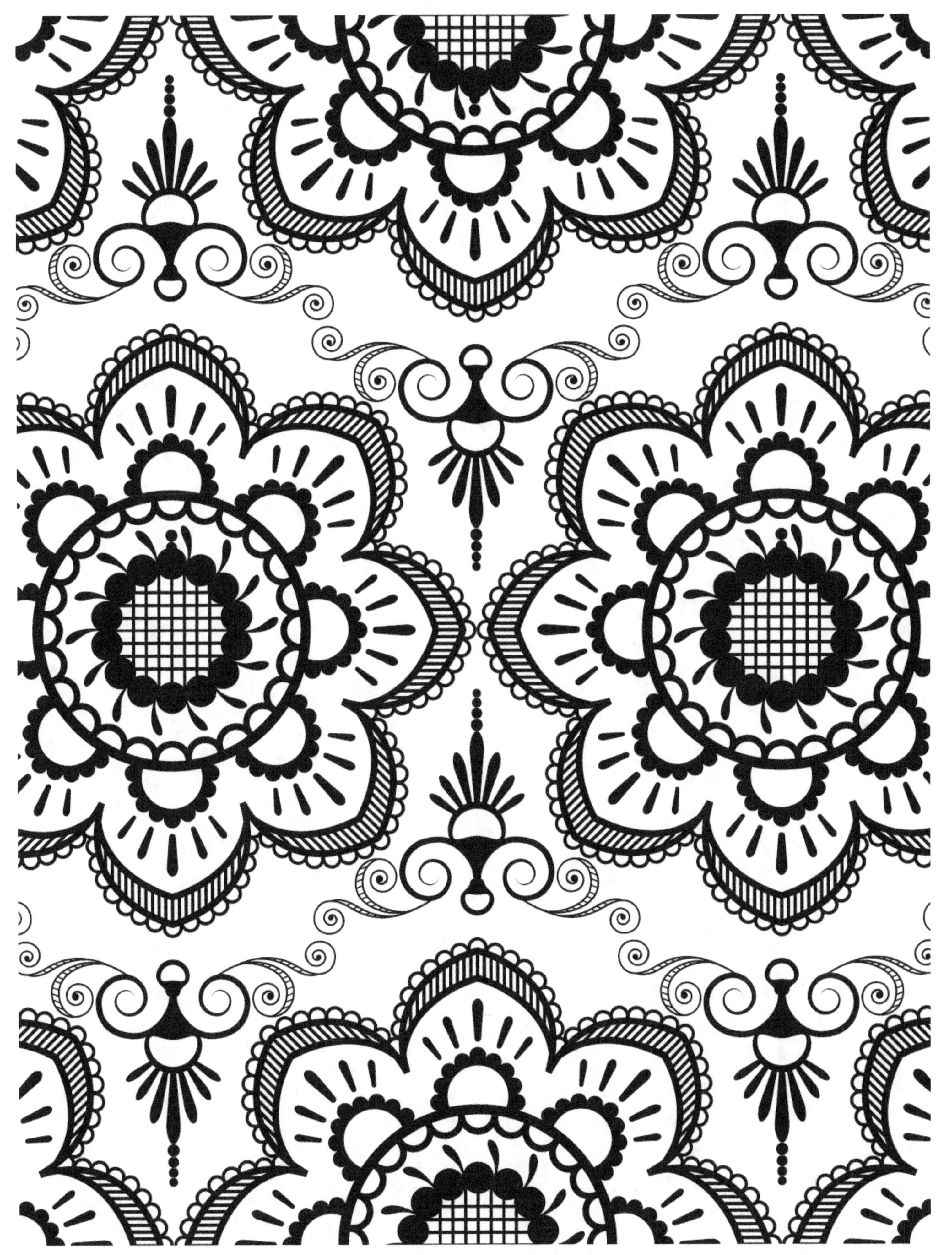

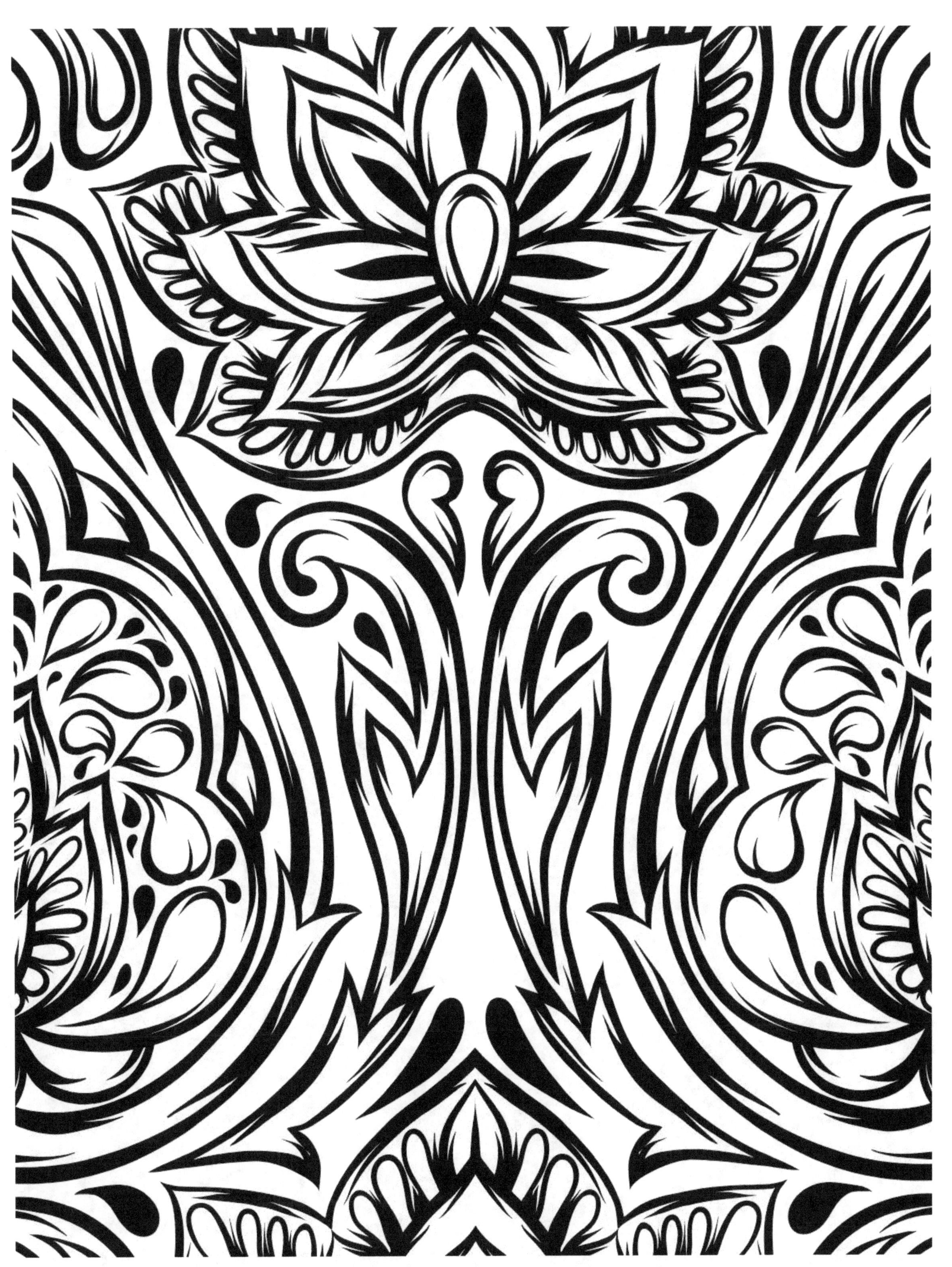

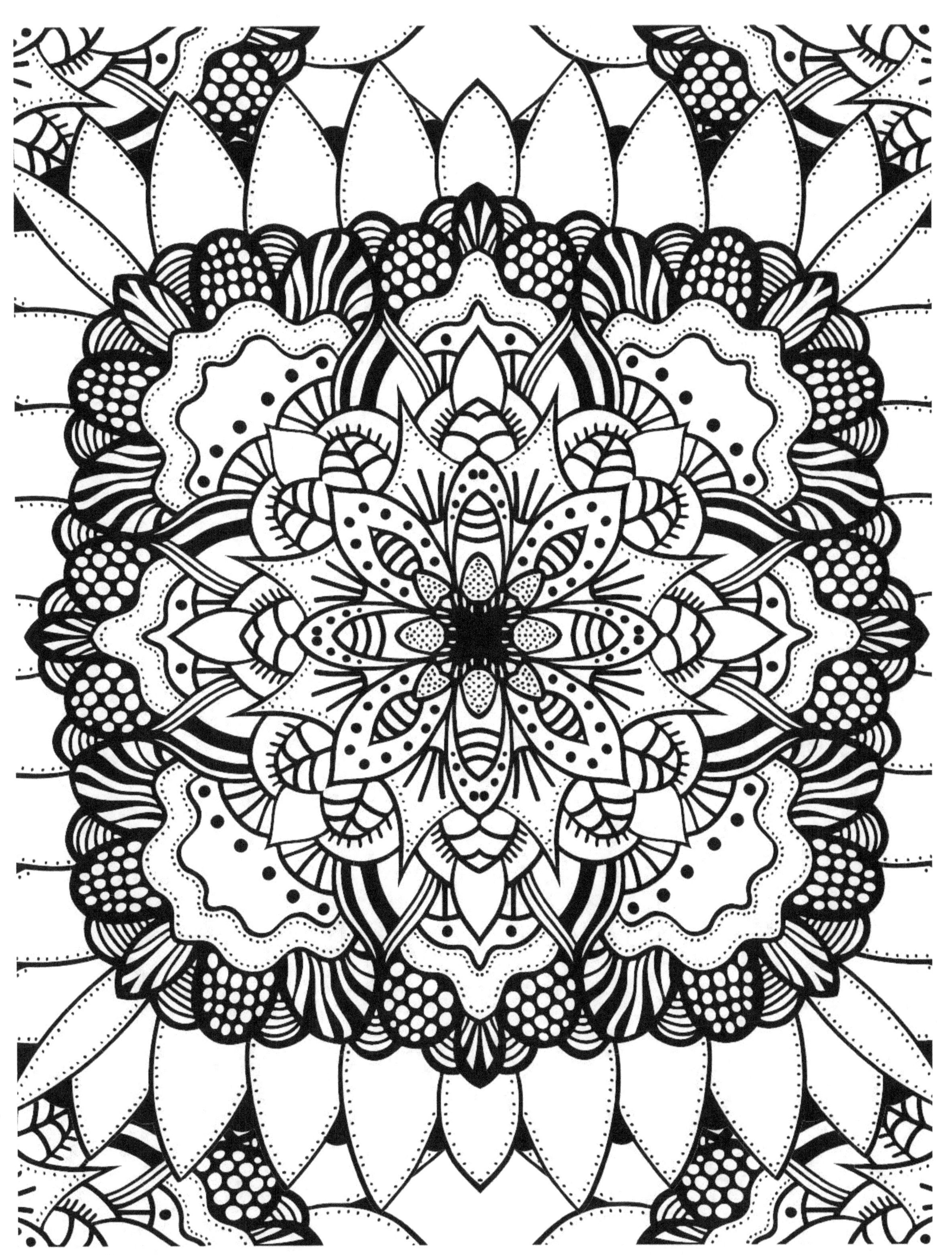

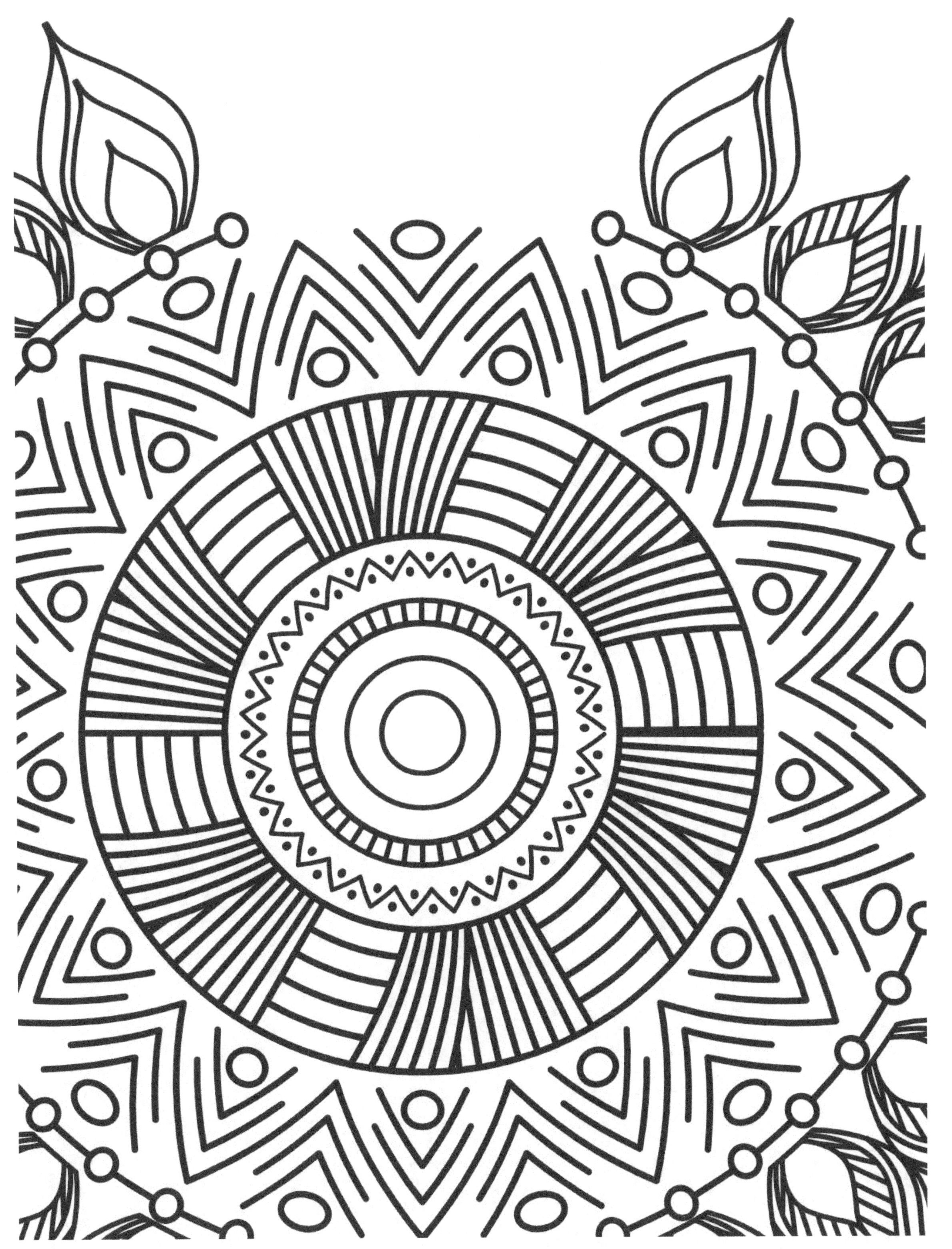

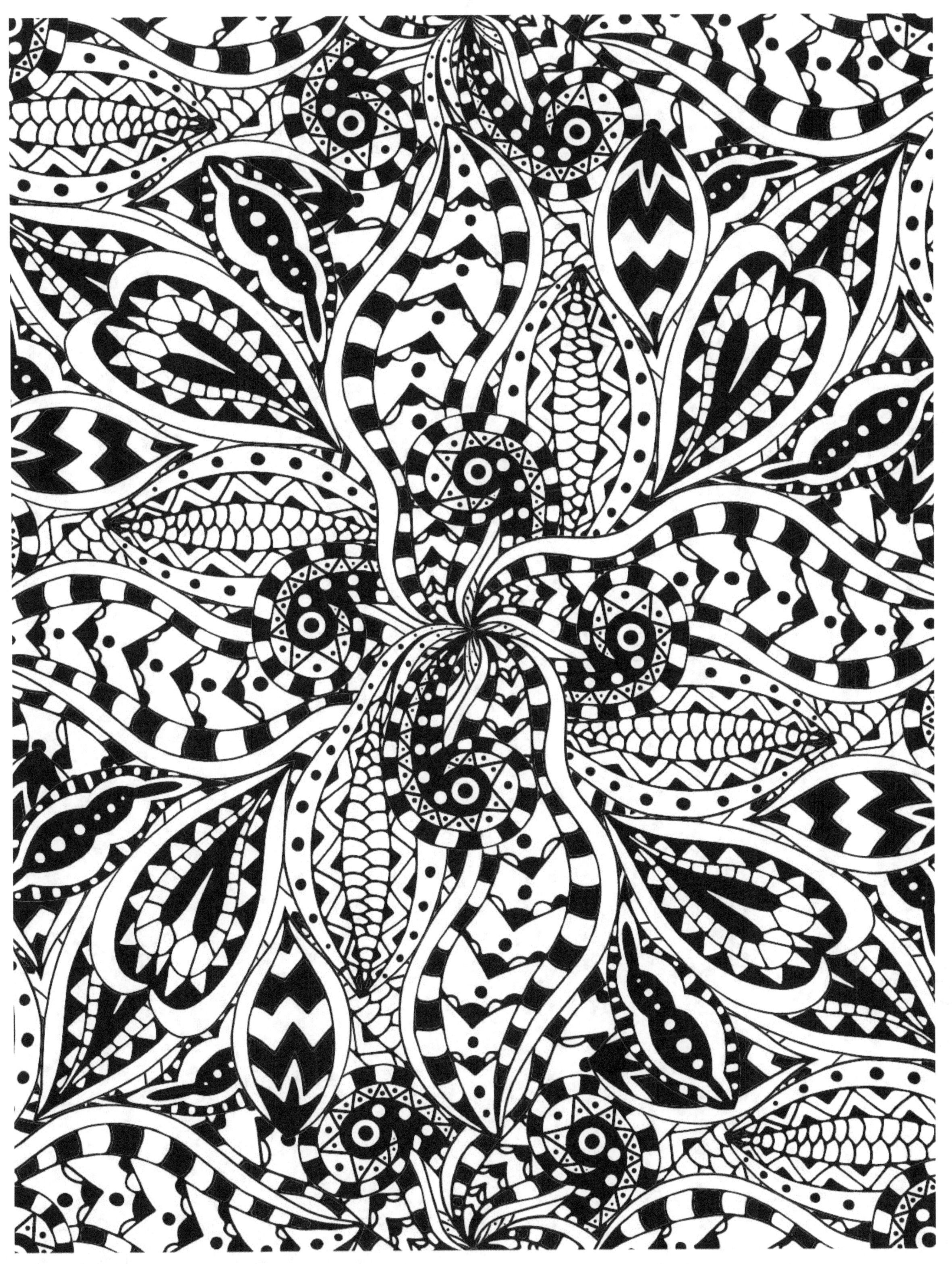

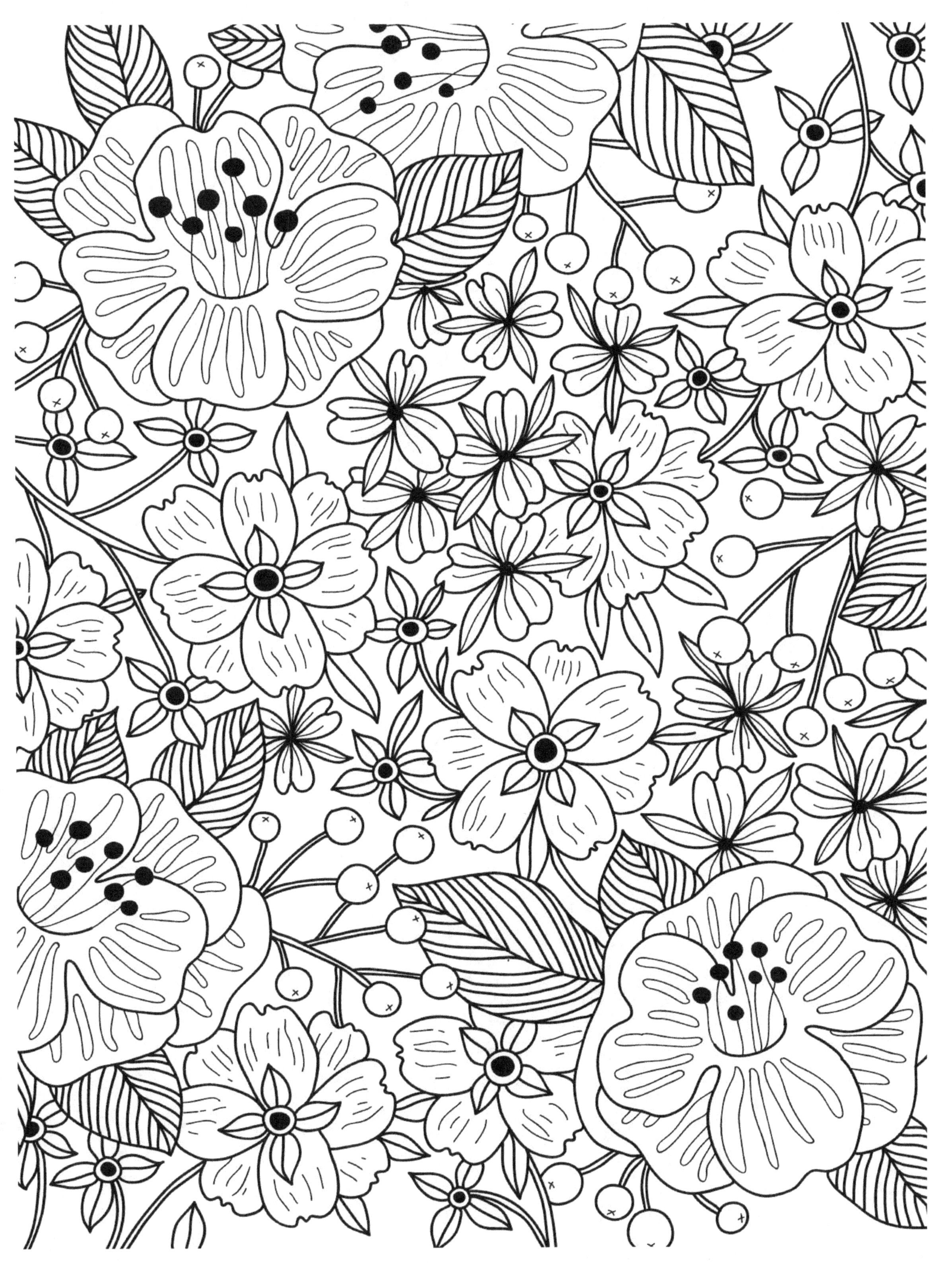

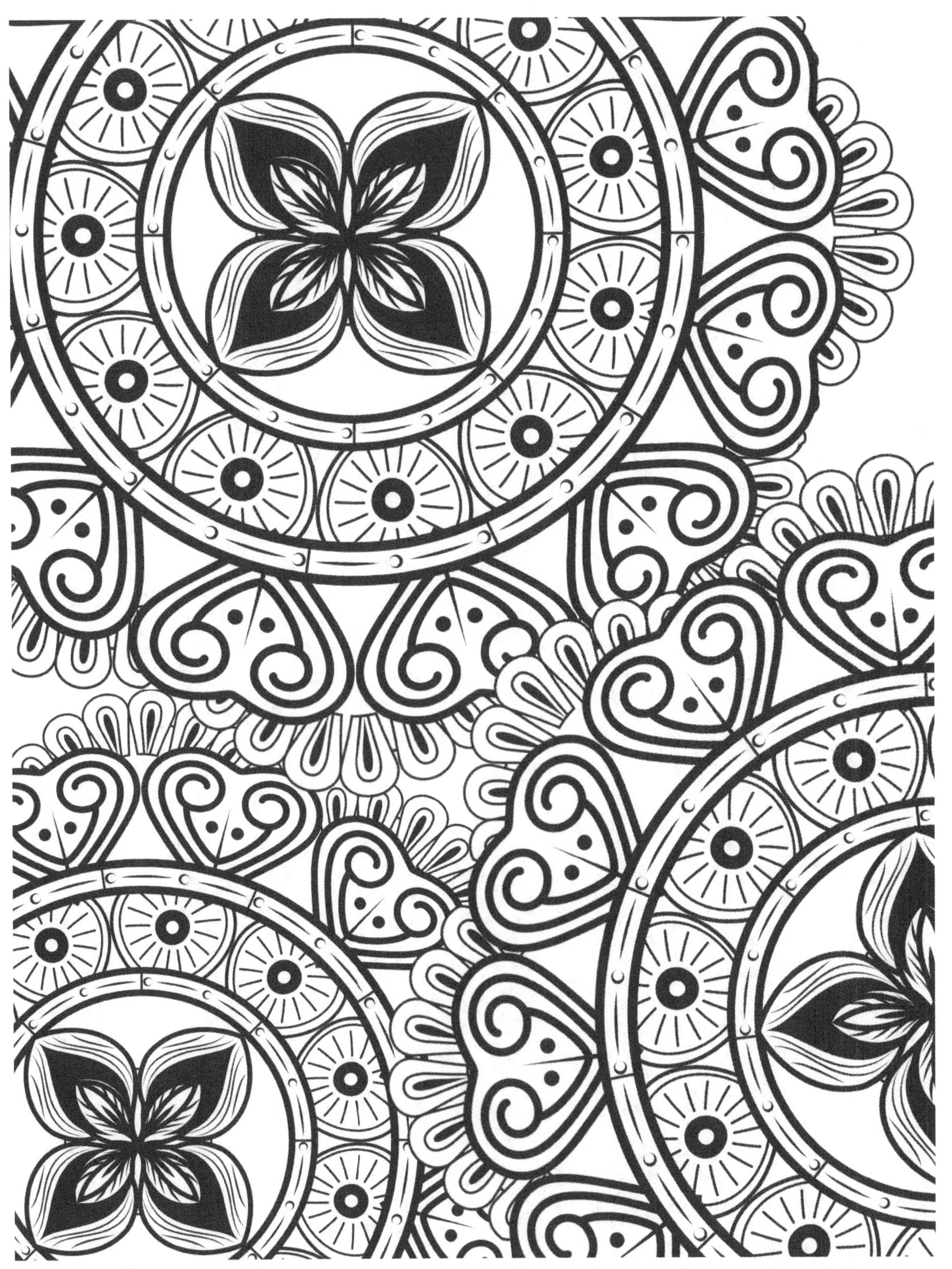

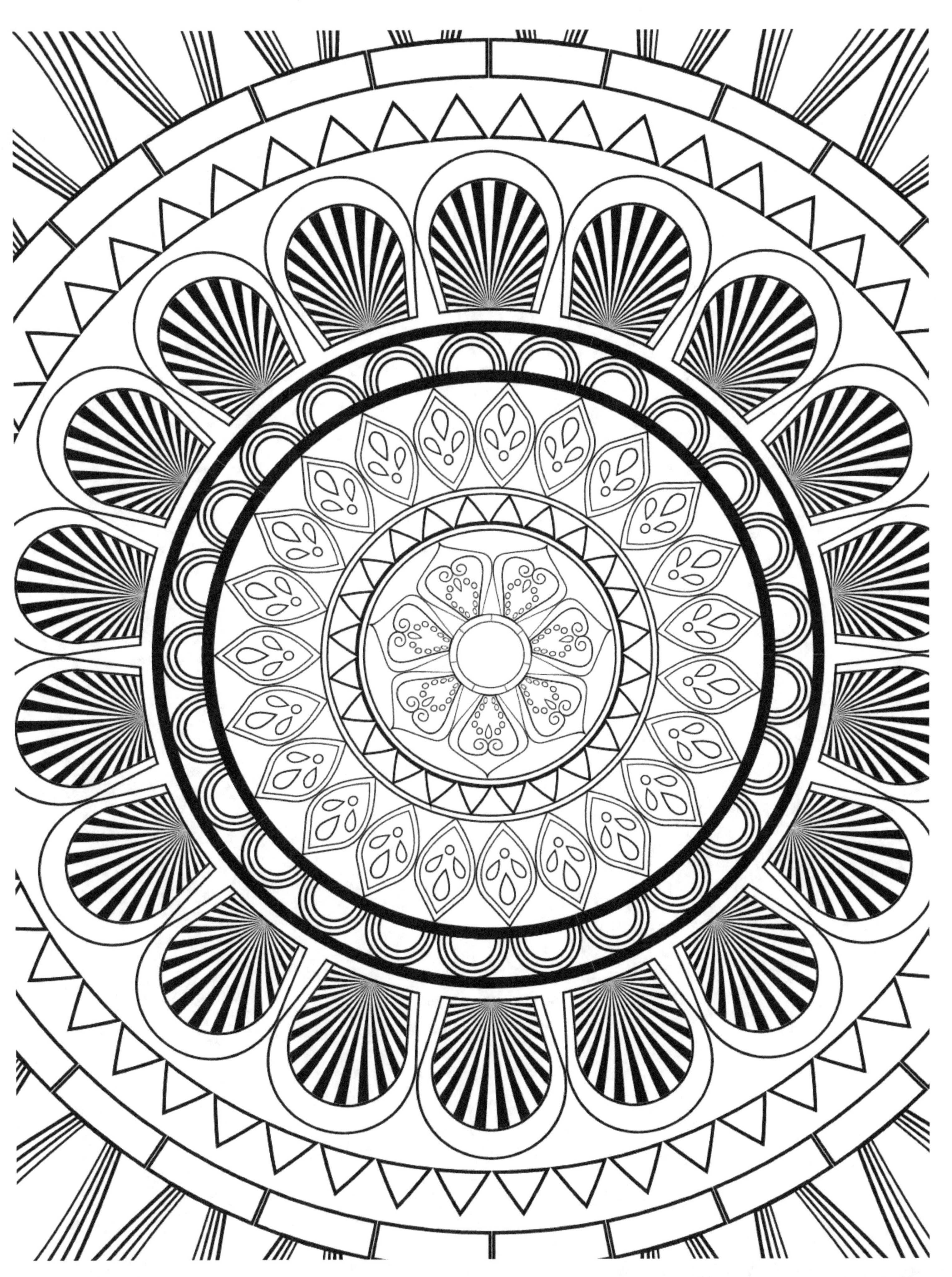

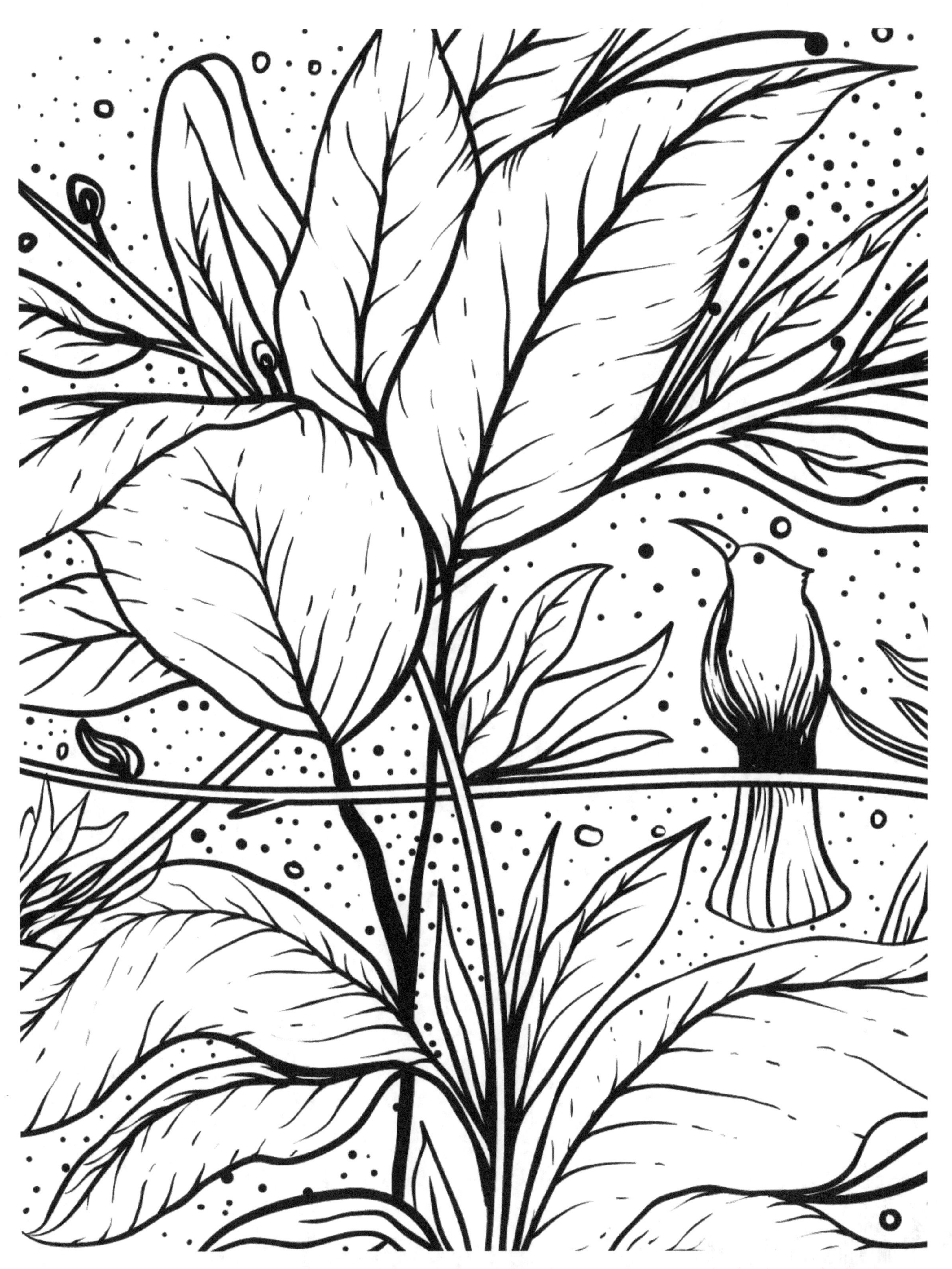